Beyond the Conservatory Model

Amid enormous changes in higher education, audience and music listener preferences, and the relevant career marketplace, music faculty are increasingly aware of the need to reimagine classical music performance training for current and future students. But how can faculty and administrators, under urgent pressure to act, be certain that their changes are effective, strategic, and beneficial for students and institutions? In this provocative yet measured book, Michael Stepniak and Peter Sirotin address these questions with perspectives rooted in extensive experience as musicians, educators, and arts leaders. Building on a multidimensional analysis of core issues and drawing upon interviews with leaders from across the performing arts and higher education music fields, Stepniak and Sirotin scrutinize arguments for and against radical change, illuminating areas of unavoidable challenge as well as areas of possibility and hope. An essential read for education leaders contemplating how classical music can continue to thrive within American higher education.

Michael Stepniak is Dean and Professor of Music at Shenandoah Conservatory of Shenandoah University. A leading arts educator and chamber musician, he holds graduate degrees in performance (Peabody Institute), musicology (Northwestern University), and education (Harvard University).

Peter Sirotin is Concertmaster of the Harrisburg Symphony Orchestra, Director of Market Square Concerts, and Artist-in-Residence at Messiah College, Pennsylvania.

CMS Emerging Fields in Music
Series Editor: Mark Rabideau
DePauw University, USA

Managing Editor: Zoua Sylvia Yang
DePauw University, USA

The *CMS Series in Emerging Fields in Music* consists of concise monographs that help the profession reimagine how we must prepare twenty-first-century musicians. Shifting cultural landscapes, emerging technologies, and a changing profession in and out of the academy demand that we reexamine our relationships with audiences, leverage our art to strengthen the communities in which we live and work, equip our students to think and act as artist-entrepreneurs, explore the limitless (and sometimes limiting) role technology plays in the life of a musician, revisit our very assumptions about what artistic excellence means and how personal creativity must be repositioned at the center of this definition, and share best practices and our own stories of successes and failures when leading institutional change.

These short-form books can be either single-authored works or contributed volumes composed of three or four essays on related topics. The books should prove useful for emerging musicians inventing the future they hope to inhabit, faculty rethinking the courses they teach and how they teach them, and administrators guiding curricular innovation and rebranding institutional identity.

Identity and Diversity in New Music
The New Complexities
Marilyn Nonken

Beyond the Conservatory Model
Reimagining Classical Music Performance Training in Higher Education
Michael Stepniak with Peter Sirotin

For more information, please visit: www.routledge.com/CMS-Emerging-Fields-in-Music/book-series/CMSEMR

Beyond the Conservatory Model

Reimagining Classical Music Performance Training in Higher Education

Michael Stepniak with
Peter Sirotin

Routledge
Taylor & Francis Group
NEW YORK AND LONDON

THE COLLEGE MUSIC SOCIETY

First published 2020
by Routledge
52 Vanderbilt Avenue, New York, NY 10017

and by Routledge
2 Park Square, Milton Park, Abingdon, Oxon, OX14 4RN

Routledge is an imprint of the Taylor & Francis Group, an informa business

© 2020 Taylor & Francis

Library of Congress Cataloging-in-Publication Data
Names: Stepniak, Michael, author. | Sirotin, Peter, author.
Title: Beyond the conservatory model : reimagining classical music
    performance training in higher education / Michael Stepniak,
    Peter Sirotin.
Description: New York : Routledge, 2019. | Series: CMS emerging
    fields in music | Includes bibliographical references and index.
Identifiers: LCCN 2019022919 (print) | LCCN 2019022920 (ebook) |
    ISBN 9780367226930 (hardback) | ISBN 9780429276415 (ebook)
Subjects: LCSH: Music in universities and colleges. | Music—
    Instruction and study. | Curriculum change.
Classification: LCC MT18 .S74 2019 (print) | LCC MT18 (ebook) |
    DDC 780.71/1—dc23
LC record available at https://lccn.loc.gov/2019022919
LC ebook record available at https://lccn.loc.gov/2019022920

ISBN: 978-0-367-22693-0 (hbk)
ISBN: 978-0-429-27641-5 (ebk)

Typeset in Sabon
by Apex CoVantage, LLC

Contents

Series Editor's Introduction

Music is embraced throughout every culture without boundaries. Today, an increasingly connected world offers influence and inspiration for opening our imaginations, as technology provides unprecedented access to global audiences. Communities gather around music to mourn collective hardships and celebrate shared moments, and every parent understands that music enhances their child's chances to succeed in life. Yet it has never been more of a struggle for musicians to make a living at their art—at least when following traditional paths.

The College Music Society's *Emerging Fields in Music Series* champions the search for solutions to the most pressing challenges and most influential opportunities presented to the music profession during this time of uncertainty and promise. This series re-examines how we as music professionals can build relationships with audiences, leverage our art to strengthen the communities in which we live and work, equip our students to think and act as artist-entrepreneurs, explore the limitless (and sometimes limiting) role technology plays in the creation and dissemination of music, revisit our very assumptions about what artistic excellence means, and share best practices and our own stories of successes and failures when leading institutional change.

These short-form books are written for emerging musicians busy inventing the future they hope to inherit, faculty rethinking the courses they teach (curriculum) and how they teach them (pedagogy), and administrators rebranding institutional identity and reshaping the student experience.

The world (and the profession) is changing. And so must we, if we are to carry forward our most beloved traditions of the past and create an audience for our best future.

Mark Rabideau

Introduction

*A time of turbulence is a dangerous time, but its
greatest danger is a temptation to deny reality.*
—Peter Drucker, *Managing in Turbulent
Times* (New York: Routledge, 2011),
p. x of Preface

*We would rather be ruined than changed,
We would rather die in our dread
Than climb the cross of the moment
And let our illusions die.*
—W. H. Auden, *The Age of Anxiety:
A Baroque Eclogue* (Princeton:
Princeton University Press,
2011), p.105

The writing of this monograph was undertaken with a nervous and far-from-certain hope. The core task—adding to currently available critiques by further illuminating the changing classical music marketplace and ways that performance training in higher education could be reimagined to better anticipate and shape that future—seemed meaningful in and of itself. But could we really illuminate a path forward that left us (and, perhaps, even our readers) hopeful?

The topics we sought to tackle were multifaceted and impervious to easy analysis. Certainly any attempt to *fully* capture the issues between our two thorny and interrelated topics—classical music and higher education—was a tad imprudent (at best). We had good reason to remember Glen Baxter's cartoon, reproduced in Image 0.1.

Ultimately, our investigative work produced rays of hope. We were moved by the willingness of higher education and music/arts industry leaders to be involved in this investigative work and are indebted to them for their generosity and openness. It is clear that the issues being investigated here mean much to many.

ALL I HAD TO DO NOW WAS
TO COAX THEM INTO THE NET

Image 0.1 G. Baxter, *Almost Completely Baxter: New and Selected Blurtings*
Source: New York: New York Review Comics, 2016, p. 100.

To confirm, we have created a monograph that employs multiple modes of analysis. It investigates issues that are disparate and often absent from discussions regarding how the academy might best save and promote the classical music artform. That is especially the case in the third chapter, where we give marked attention to the complex landscapes that higher education music faculty and leaders face when they pursue large and quick change. We give extended attention to those landscapes for a straightforward reason; our academic colleagues may have a better chance of making progress in boldly reimagining curriculum if they acknowledge and understand all that stands in the way of this work.

We know our colleagues well enough to expect that most readers (whether from higher education or music/arts industry) will bring with them a rich and nuanced understanding of a number of core concerns investigated here. We readily acknowledge that a smaller monograph—especially one that aims to connect so many typically disparate and unconnected areas of inquiry as this one—will ultimately prove inadequate to provide a full description of all core concerns. However, we hope that readers, in encountering and considering the issues in the fuller way we have sought to contextualize them here, will gain a further understanding of the challenges and opportunities we face within higher education and will even be emboldened to act on those challenges and opportunities.

We especially hope that leaders of national professional organizations—e.g., College Music Society, National Association of Schools of Music—will take further notice of the profound opportunities that remain outstanding. They are uniquely positioned to give life's blood to the work required. If they were to undertake the strategic actions outlined in chapter four, they could transform the diversity and range of music leaders within the higher education community who were skillfully oriented toward the work outlined in this volume. And in doing that, they could create a wave of needed change nationwide.

We emerge from this work further emboldened to challenge the traditional model of performance training that remains common at most higher education institutions. Let us be frank: our schools and programs have little right to continue pretending they are serving classical music performance students as well as they might in offering the type of professional preparation we typically do. Whether we higher education faculty are somewhat aware or acutely aware of the gap between our offered classical music performance training and the needs of the marketplace, the fact is that most of us *are* aware of that gap. It is long past time that we moved beyond awaiting occasional and titillating news that an individual campus or program had successfully nudged its music curriculum toward innovation and change. Those changes should be occurring nationally, and now.

A word about the layout of this volume: This monograph pursues four interrelated goals, as outlined here:

1. Reveal the current and changing classical music marketplace.
   (See chapter 1—a reworked version of a recently published article that attracted an unusually large readership—and chapter 2.)

2. Illuminate ways that the model of classical music performance training in higher education might be reimagined to align with that marketplace, enabling aspiring young musicians to better succeed in and shape that marketplace.
   (See, especially, chapter 2, which builds on an interview study with leaders from across the performing arts and higher education music fields.)

3. Acknowledge the peculiarly hostile landscape that higher education music leaders and music faculty must navigate if they are to pursue the type of bold change around classical music training that seems necessary.
   (See chapter 3.)

4. Illuminate factors that can impact the success of higher education leaders in enabling the bold change needed (as outlined in the first few chapters), and illuminate national-level action that could greatly support the success of music faculty and leaders in that work.
   (See chapter 4.)

We are perhaps most excited by the recommendations outlined in the fourth chapter. Yes, much could be gained if there were greater acceptance of the recommended (and radically reimagined) degree-level student learning outcomes outlined toward the end of chapter two. But it is the recommendations in the final chapter—aimed as they are at a radical new investment in the development of a broader and more diverse and skilled set of leaders across our field—that seem most authentic, honest, and ripe for action. Our field desperately needs the large-scale support that only our professional organizations can provide.

There is much work to be done. And if it is pursued well, our work ahead will not only be challenging but revolutionary.

Our students, surely, deserve nothing less.

We owe thanks to many. First, to our respective spouses—Anne Schempp and Ya-Ting Chang—for their indefatigable support and care. Second, to Nicole Harney, who valiantly waded through the murkiest depths of endnotes and citation formatting and emerged not only intact but cheerful on the other side. Third, to a scholar in the making, Marianna, for her keen and level-headed insights. And finally, and so important, to both Routledge Music and College Music Society. We are especially grateful to Mark Rabideau, Sylvia Yang, and Genevieve Aoki. This project would not have happened without their support and patience.

1 Beyond Beauty, Brilliance, and Expression

Musicianship and Reconnecting With the General Public[1]

Joy, Pleasures, and a Growing Discomfort

Many of us classical music performers grew up spending years apprenticing with master musicians, feeding an appetite for music making that was gloriously insatiable. We quickly grew to relish great artists and works from the past few centuries in classical music and the past century or so in jazz. The attraction was as inevitable as it was natural. Those two eras, after all, coincided with the development of extraordinary compositional and performance technique and produced musical works (and performances) that revealed moments of profound splendor and brilliance.

The fact that the increasing virtuosity and complexity of these two music genres coincided with their slowly decreasing popularity within the general public this past century didn't seem so much a fault of the music as a testament to its increasing sophistication. And our performance training—informed by tradition and focusing with rapt intent on beauty of tone, brilliance in technique, and clarity and authenticity in expression—has continued to largely ignore the awkward issue of our music's decreasing presence in the lives of those around us. Whether we were composers or performers, it was clear to us that we had a heroic charge: to propel traditions that were exceptional in their aesthetic nuance and historical significance. And we have been proud to meet that challenge, promoting art for art's sake as possible and graduating performers with often remarkable playing skills. As one prominent faculty member lamented in a recent article, it would be so wonderful if we could support the development of young musicians who enter higher education with an unconditional love for music by providing them with a learning and teaching environment relative free of the myriad practical concerns related to marketplace and career pathways.[2]

We have sought to pursue art for art's sake even while being part of institutions and educational systems endlessly ravenous for more tuition revenue, endlessly ravenous for more and better pupils to fill ensembles, courses, programs, and faculty loads.[3] The joy and pleasures of classical and jazz music have been virtually boundless for most of us "in the know." And for those of us fortunate to work within educational communities boasting exceptional performance series, that joy is ongoing. I think of a number of standout performances within my own conservatory during the past couple of years—the breathtaking honesty and intensity of Gidon Kremer and Kremerata Baltica, the spellbinding inventiveness of Cecile McLorin Salvant, the virtuosic whimsy of Roomful of Teeth. Most readers will have their own examples.

All this said, I must admit a discomfort that seems to have reached a tipping point; a discomfort with the dichotomy between these joyful experiences and two stubborn realities: the ever-increasing employment challenges facing our graduating music performance students and the relative unpopularity of these two musical genres among the general public. In having to repeatedly consider the issues, I've come to an uncomfortable conclusion: beyond all their extraordinary splendor, the cultures surrounding our two music performance disciplines—the "art music" genres long privileged in our conservatories and college/university music departments—have come to contain a small and pernicious quality. That pernicious quality, one further exacerbated by the peculiar pressures within our higher education system as outlined earlier and in the next chapter, might be described as follows: thrilled by beauty and brilliance and by the aesthetic experiences accessible to us fortunate few, we increasingly adopted an attitude that cared little for one additional critical component of musicianship (at least as understood long ago): *the interest to connect with and move the average general-public listener*. The cost of that inherited mindset among both composers and performers, of our "not caring if you listen," has been nothing short of devastating.

Consider that never in human history have people had easier access to music. As studies such as Nielsen's *2017 Music 360 Report* reveal, thanks in part to the advance of streaming technology platforms, the general population of the United States over the age of 13 listens to music in excess of 32 hours weekly.[4] (That average of 32 hours of listening per week is up from an average of 26.6 and 23.2 hours for 2016 and 2015, respectively.) While there is broad engagement with music, there are two musical genres that have increasingly moved to the periphery of ordinary life, the very two genres that I would argue have become unusually comfortable ignoring emotional connection between music performer and the general-public listener. It should come as no surprise when we learn (as we do annually now from the *Nielsen Music Year End Report*) that public consumption of classical or jazz music recordings now typically hovers at around 1 percent of such consumption. As the jazz pianist Bill Anschell bluntly explained with only slight exaggeration, "People who want to play jazz actually outnumber those who enjoy or even tolerate it, let alone pay to hear it."[5] The decline has been a long time coming. While many of the data regarding classical audience size in the early twentieth century are anecdotal, it seems clear that when it came to radio audience preferences and record industry sales, classical music and jazz were a major force. As Russell Sanjek reported in his well-researched book, "semiclassical and classical" programming occupied nearly 70 percent of program time of network-created radio programming in the late 1920s and early 1930s,[6] and the sale of classical records represented almost 35 percent of industry sales in 1952.[7]

To be sure, there have been music leaders in the academy along the way who have urged us to pay more attention to the general marketplace. I think immediately of Peter Schoenbach's argument to the National Association of Schools of Music in 1999 that we must pay more heed to the connection between music performance training and careers available to our students.[8] And I think of the ongoing blogs of such change-advocates and arts leaders as Greg Sandow.[9] In the more recent past, our schools have increasingly responded by tweaking the edges of curriculum (while retaining core courses and traditional apprenticeship models): new courses for students in social media branding, marketing, entrepreneurship! Using the breathless language that is commonplace around higher education marketing, we've typically announced any tweaks to curriculum as revolutionary or innovative even while they largely remain, in the words of one exceptional CMS Task Force, little more than a "scattering of new offerings atop an unchanging foundation."[10]

Caught between performance faculty largely uninterested in pursuing any profound curricular changes that could seemingly threaten the shared value of art for art's sake and a marketplace increasingly disinterested in our graduating students and their musical skills, many of us higher education leaders have replied to the unpopularity issue with a sigh. It is easy for us to lament the many external reasons jazz and classical music have become tied for least popular musical genre. Tops among the culprits we can easily list are the following: diminishing attention spans; the proliferation of entertainment options for audiences; the greatly increased presence of creative energy and inventiveness in popular entertainment; and the worse-than-ever level of pre-college education (including general music education).

Again, many of our performance-oriented artist faculty have remained less concerned about these realities. Their viewpoint is understandable. Buoyed by the success that they and their most fortunate student performers have had and continue to have as performers within major venues, buoyed by a well-developed and reliable audience base for traditional programing within their own institutions, and having in front of them a repertoire and discipline worthy of lifelong examination, why should they care much about issues of general popularity or the employment marketplace facing the typical graduating music performer? It's a question that tuition-paying parents of those same graduating students are more than happy to answer.

Ways We in Higher Education May Help

It almost goes without saying that the most responsible reaction to a changed marketplace with extraordinarily limited full-time employment opportunities for our graduates would be not only to train our students differently but *to also train far fewer of them.* But there are too many compelling justifications to continue the status quo. No, it is unlikely that we will pursue any reduction in the number of music performance programs, faculty, and students voluntarily. So what are ways we in higher education could help this state of affairs?

At the most superficial level, a reshaped definition of musicianship would require us to fundamentally reshape general BM/MM/DMA performance degrees, not only to continue to support the development and promotion of exceptional artistry (we *must* stand for that) but also to help strengthen the orientation of our young musicians toward connection-making.[11] But this enlarged definition of musicianship would, in fact, require us to rethink virtually every area of our operations and work.

Before turning to some of the most significant areas that would require our rethinking, a side note is worth mentioning here. If our shared working definition of musicianship included a central concern with connecting with general-public listeners, we would also likely begin to impact and strengthen the relevance of our cherished artforms to the world around us. As we're reminded weekly, this additional concern of connection with general-public listeners is being embraced by an extraordinary array of forward-looking professional ensembles and companies—consider the experiments of Opera Philadelphia or California Symphony for just two recent examples.

The adoption of an enlarged definition of musicianship (as described earlier) would create urgency for change across our entire curriculum and workplace. The following list of changes and strategies are illustrative of what we could and would need to pursue. To be clear, even the full employment of all these listed changes would not radically improve the popularity of our musical genres or ease the tough employment landscape facing our graduating students anytime soon. Given the state of things, however, we must do more to get things moving in the right direction.

To begin with, this enlarged concept of musicianship would force our music schools to reimagine all aspects of our current apprenticeship model. We would need to ensure that student performance evaluations in all our undergraduate and graduate performance degrees—in end-of-semester juries, sophomore screenings, recitals, and the like—focused not only on how well a student sounded and played/sang but to what extent she was able to connect with and engage members of the general public in and through her musical performance. I think here of teachers like Midori who push students to perform in unorthodox spaces in front of ordinary people, learning along the way how to engage and communicate meaningfully with fellow human beings. (Even this approach—hardly radical to be sure—remains far outside the norm in our conservatories and music schools.)

Yes, this would require the need to develop new evaluation methods. Our music schools have multiple ways of measuring how well a student sounds and plays/sings, but we certainly don't have robust ways to measure a student's achievement in "attracting and engaging members of the general public." And we would need to be mindful that an initial positive reaction to a performance by the general public is not the sole marker of success; we would also need to help young musicians learn how to build *longer-term* engagement with new audiences and would need to figure out how to evaluate that capacity and skill. Creating a relevant evaluation tool would be exceptionally difficult but likely not impossible. Of course, some may be scandalized by the idea of attempts to assess something so extraordinarily personal and subjective. But if we are to evaluate music performance in the academy (and it seems we must), shouldn't we be taking honest steps to evaluate what has long been one of the chief aims of music making, namely, the ability to connect with and move an ordinary fellow human being?

I beg the reader's patience to consider an anecdote that might illuminate this further. A few months ago, I was chatting with a musician

I've admired for decades. Beyond being one of the leading jazz and classical performers of our time, he directs a top conservatory-based jazz program. While talking about the latest crop of new students, he paused to reflect on one audition this year that particularly stood out for him and his faculty. He described (with ongoing fascination) what happened at the end of that audition. I paraphrase: "My faculty always have a lot to say. But after this kid played, well, no one was saying a thing. And I asked him—this kid from [a northern European country]—'where did you learn to play like that?' He talked about having grown up listening to various recordings of major jazz artists and feeling the music as they felt it. I asked him again, 'Yeah, but how did you learn to play *like that*?' The kid finally explained that for the past few years, he and a couple of his friends would regularly go to nursing homes and other small venues and perform in front of people in his community." The point was clear: this student's performance evidenced more than just beauty and brilliance and skill in expression; it revealed a richly developed sensitivity to connecting with fellow human beings. It was a sensitivity made possible by his pursuit of a path far outside the norm of how we train and evaluate musicians. It is precisely *that* quality that I am suggesting we help promote, including (especially) during moments of formal assessment.

Related to this strategy, we could reshape hiring practices. Hiring decisions for typical performance faculty would likely need to increasingly incorporate questions such as "how will this applicant strengthen our ability to train musicians who might not only perform brilliantly but also connect with general members of the public?" Our investment in strengthening connection to members of a diverse population would also certainly require a greater commitment to diversity and inclusion. (Yes, classical music in particular continues to have a diversity problem.) And a relevant hiring question would certainly be "How will this faculty or staff applicant help strengthen our commitment to excellence, including inclusion and diversity?"

It might be too obvious to state, but our efforts to tackle this issue seriously would likely fail without us better ensuring that performance students received regular mentorship from and had access to internships with specific types of artists (both regular faculty and others); artists who were not only committed to the heritage and future of their musical genre, but were also skilled in effectively building programs of great music (whether old or new) to engage members of the general public where they were. Those locations might include places such as schools or retirement homes, community centers or hospitals for children, pubs or libraries.

I mention children for a specific reason. For too long, our conservatories and music schools have perceived the hard work of imagining and creating meaningful musical experiences for families and children as (at best) a distraction from the central work of developing artistry. There are many artists who are making strides in this area. One thinks, for example, of Orli Shaham's Baby Got Bach concert series, the family-oriented performances delivered by groups such as the extraordinary reed quintet Calefax, or the outreach efforts for younger people by Jazz at Lincoln Center. Given the need to build audiences and the paucity of music in public schools across this country, it's past time we helped more of our undergraduate and graduate students develop skills relevant to the joyful and difficult work of connecting with young audiences. We should not assume that all students have an interest in focusing on children or family programming, but more of our students deserve an opportunity to develop skillfulness in that area.

Advancement toward this goal would probably also require us to be more diligent in building strategic and three-way partnerships between our schools and those artists and arts presenting organizations that share a dedication to beauty, brilliance, and music's capacity to communicate to and move the person with no classical/jazz experience or training. There are many such presenting organizations and artists around. As my own conservatory has learned working with certain artists and the nearby Washington Performing Arts or the Ryuji Ueno Foundation, that type of triple partnership provides many benefits, ranging from opportunities for more authentic connection making with regional communities to financial advantages for all.

It also seems foolhardy for us to graduate students who are skilled *only* as live performance artists given that the general public is increasingly listening to music recordings, especially through on-demand audio streaming (up 59 percent between 2016 and 2017 alone[12] and now accounting for at least two-thirds of U.S. music industry revenue).[13] As Panos Panay wrote a number of years ago, predicting audience trends, "music listeners are moving away from the mass-produced music consumption habits of the broadcast media to the more tailored and personalized experiences of the social media age."[14] Given the public's strong and growing interest in recorded and streaming music, it seems important that we ensure our graduating classical music and jazz performance students have familiarity not only with delivering a powerful live performance (and marketing same) but with creating and promoting powerful recorded performances.[15] The technology related to recording and distributing recorded music has become extraordinarily accessible. Adding such a component to the training of aspiring music performers would certainly not require significant credit space in the curriculum.

We would likely also need to make hiring and funding decisions for music ensembles with a greater eye to impact connection-making. Music schools and programs that elevated human connection to a central value in musicianship training would certainly be interested to judge the success of a training orchestra or jazz ensemble (and its director) not only according to how well it executed a repertoire/program, but also regarding how successful its programming and performance was in attracting and connecting with new audience members from the surrounding local region. Without diminishing commitment to technical excellence and artistry, ensemble directors and leaders would be challenged to assume a new and central role in strengthening the impact and relevance of our music to those around.

And, yes, the pursuit of the radical change being considered here would require us to better help undergraduate and graduate students develop relevant and practical marketing and business skills. There is much that competes for our attention in contemporary living. And as we're constantly reminded, the contemporary marketplace especially rewards technological savviness, marketing acumen, and the ability to utilize social media and online platforms.

Music performance artists newly making their way in the world would also greatly benefit from having such finance-oriented skills as the ability to court donors, the ability to pursue successful grant writing, and the sensitivity to ensure artist branding and images effectively capture the attention of an increasingly visual-dominated marketplace. To be sure, these added areas of instruction and learning typically lie outside the expertise of music faculty. The opportunity exists, then, for us to further build organic partnerships with cutting-edge programs and faculty in business and marketing programs at our universities and colleges. That type of collaboration and expertise-sharing could be of great value to our schools. After all, not only is it an effective way to strengthen the preparation of our students for professional success and provide them with additional skills of value in the contemporary marketplace, but also it can also help us realize further expense sharing.

Some Likely Criticisms

I know that colleagues may well have criticisms of what has been outlined and proposed.[16]

Some heads of future-oriented institutions might well argue that their institutions are in fact making good progress in helping graduates better navigate an extraordinarily challenging marketplace that cares quite little for our music. One thinks, for example, of the long-standing efforts at Eastman School of Music or DePauw's unusually compre-hensive 21st Century Musician Initiative. Or the multiple initiatives being pursued in music areas at SMU, USC, Oberlin, NEC, Peabody, Juilliard, and elsewhere (including my own school). While helpful, the strategies being currently promoted and undertaken in many schools, I would argue, don't go anywhere far enough. Pursuing changes largely limited to the edges of curriculum, they do not truly get at the core of what needs fixing.

The individual passionate about traditional repertoire and the integ-rity of either of the two musical genres we are considering may cer-tainly be wondering whether the proposed changes, focused as they are on the interest of members of the general public, wouldn't simply end up producing crossover artists; young creative types who titillated general audiences with music that represented watered-down versions of multiple styles. The question and the related concern are perhaps understandable. Many professional orchestras and music organiza-tions, after all, have resorted to presenting that very type of music in the name of attracting new ticket-purchasing audience members. (I hesitate to give examples here.) The concern for our students, how-ever, is likely misplaced. They bring with them an exceptional range of interests and sensitivities. Yes, some might end up becoming crossover artists. But many—*if mentored by faculty possessing those very same values and goals*—would likely remain invested in their musical heri-tage and repertoire. Perhaps most important, a much greater number of young musicians would be leaving our training programs with the very qualities we find present in the musicians we most admire—a powerfully authentic and individual musical voice.

Other readers may be dismissive of core aspects of our argument, pointing out that artist-teachers in our music schools and conservato-ries have in fact *long* focused on connection making. After all, those readers might posit, our performance faculty typically give marked attention to a student's skill to communicate a mood or idea clearly through her singing or playing. That contention is true but misses the mark. Expression is no substitute for connection of the type advocated here, where what is prized is not only a performer's clear expression but his or her interest in the general-public listener's engagement and emotional response. Again, I would argue that our training and appren-ticeship model in classical and jazz performance pays little attention to the orientation or attitude of the performer toward listeners unfa-miliar with our exceptionally-developed musical genres. Indeed, the degree of a performer's aloofness or disinterest in the experience of the general-public listener is typically assumed to be largely irrelevant to the judged quality of the related music performance. The clearest expression of that assumption is found in our primary methods of performance evaluation—whether beginning-of-semester ensemble auditions, jury rubrics, recital evaluations, or studio grades—virtually none of which evaluate a performer's interest or ability to connect with general-public listeners.

Still other readers may be asserting that now is the most extraordinary of times for our two music genres and that the concerns raised here are of the hyperbolic "sky-is-falling" variety. To be clear, I am as hesitant to admit our situation is hopeless as I am unable to claim it is free of pernicious flaws. (To be fair, it is much too complicated to be described in any straightforward way.) I certainly agree with Nate Chinen, who asserts in his recent book that when it comes to jazz artists/creators we are within a moment of abundance, surrounded by an explosion of new techniques and accents.[17] And, like many fellow classical musicians, I read with some interest the energetic exchange a few years ago between Greg Sandow and Heather Mac Donald (as carried out in Sandow's Arts Journal blog and Mac Donald's writing in *City Journal*).[18] As readers here likely know, their argument outlined two seemingly opposite positions: that classical music was dangerously in decline (Sandow) or in a golden era (Mac Donald). I was one of those who agreed with a fair bit of the argument on both sides. We have done well in the academy to highlight and contribute to the latter quality—at no time has the performance level been greater or pursued by a greater variety of ensembles and performers in more locales. But we have been far less courageous in admitting to the former.

Other readers might be questioning the relevance and viability of the strategies proposed for our conservatories and most focused young performers. I agree that a tiny portion of our young and sometimes most gifted musicians have limited ability to connect with others and give attention to what others around them think and feel. Given their potential capacity to also enrich our musical landscape, there is strong argument for keeping their training as is. And a highly specialized degree such as the Artist Diploma certainly offers those extremely rare students best support, allowing them to focus squarely on their instruments and repertoire.

The great majority of our young and gifted musicians, however, seem entirely prepared to learn and thrive within music programs that would newly dedicate themselves to beauty, brilliance, expression, *and music's capacity for building human connection*. Indeed, we shouldn't underestimate the capacity of these students to be thought leaders in this work. As a cherished friend and veteran music school leader recently reflected, "we can take comfort in the fact that more young people today want to engage in meaningful music making than in any time in history." Note that he wasn't referencing faculty or our current model of instruction. His point was that an unusual percentage of *students* seem ready to address the challenges our genres face. We can and must support them better.

Our Students

In the end, the quality and the character of our students are perhaps the greatest sources of hope for the futures of these two musical genres. Yes, a not insignificant portion of our conservatory and music school faculty likely understand the dire circumstances surrounding our musical genres. And some of them would no doubt be willing to embrace the considerable challenge of enlarging our definition of musicianship and adding the new core value to their work, helping to begin strengthening the relevance of our musical genres to everyday life. Their willingness to radically overhaul entire curricula would, of course, be vital to any progress. I strongly believe that the extraordinary difficulty of their work would be more than matched by the readiness of our young musicians to tackle the issue described here. Beyond bringing great passion for their music, they bring a readiness and interest to newly invest in human interconnectedness.

To put it simply, we are surrounded by a next generation ready to play a key role in strengthening the relevance of our cherished musical genres to those around. We can and must do better to support them in that task.

Notes

1. A version of this chapter originally appeared in *College Music Symposium* (Vol. 57, September 6, 2017) as an article by Michael Stepniak titled "Beauty, Brilliance, and Expression: On Reimagining Jazz and Classical Music Performance Training & Reconnecting with the General Public." It appears here in a revised version with the permission of the College Music Society: https://symposium.music.org/index.php?option=com_k2&view=item&id=11353:beyond-beauty-brilliance-and-expression-on-reimagining-jazz-and-classical-music-performance-training-reconnecting-with-the-general-public&Itemid=126, accessed September 3, 2018.
2. See Atar Arad's article "Atar Arad on Orchestra Excerpts & the Unconditional Love of Music," *Strings*, August 15, 2017, http://stringsmagazine.com/atar-arad-orchestra/, accessed September 3, 2018.

3. Like cogs in wheels within wheels, it is easy for us to avoid moral responsibility for the overabundance of graduates entering our professional fields.
4. The full report can be found at https://a2im.org/downloads/Nielsen_U.S._Music_360_HighlightsFINAL.pdf. For a summary, see www.nielsen.com/us/en/insights/news/2017/time-with-tunes-how-technology-is-driving-music-consumption.html, accessed September 3, 2018.
5. B. Anschell, "Jazz Careers," *All About Jazz*, June 17, 2012. The article, aimed at provoking a field overflowing with talent, certainly hit a nerve. It can be found online at www.allaboutjazz.com/careers-in-jazz-by-bill-anschell.php, accessed September 3, 2018.
6. R. Sanjek, *American Popular Music and Its Business: The First Four Hundred Years* (New York: Oxford University Press, 1988), 87.
7. R. Sanjek, *American Popular Music and Its Business*, 244.
8. P. Schoenbach, "Career Preparation: Moving into the American Marketplace with the Bachelor of Music in Performance: Innovation and New Thoughts about Performance Training for the Future," *Proceedings, the 75th Annual Meeting, 1999* (Reston, VA: National Association of Schools of Music, 2000), 6–11.
9. For examples of Sandow's arguments and advocacy, see his blog www.artsjournal.com/sandow/, accessed September 3, 2018.
10. D. Myers, E. Sarath, J. Chattah, L. Higgins, V. Levine, D. Rudge, and T. Rice, *Transforming Music Study From Its Foundations: A Manifesto for Progressive Change in the Undergraduate Preparation of Music Majors Report of the Task Force on the Undergraduate Music Major*, College Music Society, November 2014, 16, www.mtosmt.org/issues/mto.16.22.1/manifesto.pdf, accessed September 2, 2018.
11. The potential role of the Artist Diploma degree is discussed later in this chapter.
12. That Nielsen report is accessible for download at www.nielsen.com/us/en/insights/reports/2018/2017-music-us-year-end-report.html, accessed September 4, 2018. For a wonderful graphical representation of how the U.S. public's consumption has changed between 1973 and 2017 when it comes to recorded music format, see the chart provided by Recording Industry Association of America at www.riaa.com/u-s-sales-database/, accessed September 4, 2018.
13. See the Recording Industry Association of America's *News and Notes on 2017 RIAA Revenue Statistics* report, www.riaa.com/wp-content/uploads/2018/03/RIAA-Year-End-2017-News-and-Notes.pdf, accessed September 4, 2018.
14. P. Panay, "Rethinking Music: The Future of Making Money as a Performing Artist," in *Rethinking Music: A Briefing Book* (Boston: Berkman Center for Internet & Society, 2011), 59, https://cyber.harvard.edu/sites/cyber.harvard.edu/files/Rethinking_Music_Briefing_Book_April-25-2011.pdf, accessed September 4, 2018.
15. To confirm, the experience of live performance should be promoted and advanced; there is, after all, little that matches live performance as a shared and communal human experience. But that promotion and advancement should also be accompanied by an acknowledgment of the size of the marketplace that listens to recorded music, including through audio streaming.

16. For practical purposes, only a handful of the more likely areas of disagreement are discussed here. As many readers will understand, the issues relevant to this topic are of stunning variety and number.
17. N. Chinen, *Playing Changes: Jazz for the New Century* (New York: Pantheon Books, 2018).
18. The back and forth began with Mac Donald's publishing *Classical Music's New Golden Age* on July 20, 2010, at city-journal.org. Greg Sandow quickly published five responses on his Arts Journal blog, beginning with *Cockeyed Optimist* on July 25, 2010, then *Off in the Clouds* on July 27, 2010, then *Still in the Clouds* on July 29, 2010, then *The Poor Dead Horse* on July 30, 2010, and finally *One Last Thought . . .* on July 30, 2010. Mac Donald's response to Sandow's responses appeared at city-journal.org on August 100, 2010, as *The Unsustainable Declinism of Greg Sandow*.

Bibliography

2017 U.S. Music Year-End Report. Report. Music, Nielsen. New York, NY: Nielsen Company, 2018. Accessed September 5, 2018. www.nielsen.com/us/en/insights/reports/2018/2017-music-us-year-end-report.html.

Albright, D. "The Evolution of Music Consumption: How We Got Here." *MakeUseOf*, April 30, 2015. Accessed September 6, 2018. www.makeuseof.com/tag/the-evolution-of-music-consumption-how-we-got-here/.

Anschell, B. "Jazz Careers." *All About Jazz*, June 17, 2012. Accessed September 5, 2018. www.allaboutjazz.com/careers-in-jazz-by-bill-anschell.php.

Arad, A. "Atar Arad on Orchestra Excerpts & the Unconditional Love of Music." *Strings* 32, no. 1 (August 15, 2017): 36–38.

"Bachelor of Music Degree Programs." *Eastman School of Music*. Accessed September 5, 2018. www.esm.rochester.edu/admissions/ugrad/bm/.

Beckman, G.D. "'Adventuring' Arts Entrepreneurship Curricula in Higher Education: An Examination of Present Efforts, Obstacles, and Best Practices." *Journal of Arts Management, Law, and Society* 37, no. 2 (Summer, 2007): 87–112.

"The Breakthrough Plan." *Peabody Conservatory*, June 2018. Accessed September 5, 2018. https://peabody.jhu.edu/explore-peabody/our-future/breakthrough-plan/.

Brown, Alan S. *Classical Music Consumer Segmentation Study*. Report. John S. and James L. Knight Foundation, University of Rochester. Southport, CT: Audience Insight LLC, 2002.

"Center for Innovation in the Arts at the Juilliard School." *The Juilliard School*. Accessed September 5, 2018. www.juilliard.edu/school/academics/center-innovation-arts.

"Center for Teaching Innovation and Excellence." *Oberlin College and Conservatory*. Accessed September 5, 2018. http://languages.oberlin.edu/blogs/ctie/tag/curriculum/.

Chinen, N. *Playing Changes: Jazz for the New Century*. New York: Pantheon Books, 2018.

"Conservatory Areas of Study." *Oberlin College and Conservatory.* August 29, 2018. Accessed September 5, 2018. www.oberlin.edu/conservatory/areas-of-study.

"Conservatory Learning Goals and Outcomes." *Oberlin College and Conservatory*, September 4, 2018. Accessed September 5, 2018. www.oberlin.edu/dean-of-the-conservatory/learning-goals-and-outcomes.

Crawford, E. *Nielsen Music Year-End Report U.S. 2016.* Report. Music, Nielsen. New York, NY: Nielsen Company, 2017.

Crawford, E. *U.S. Music 360: 2017 Report Highlights.* Report. Music, Nielsen. New York, NY: Nielsen Company, 2017. Accessed September 5, 2018. https://a2im.org/downloads/Nielsen_U.S._Music_360_Highlights FINAL.pdf.

A Decade of Arts Engagement: Findings from the Survey of Public Participation in the Arts, 2002–2012. Report no. 58. National Endowment for the Arts. Washington, DC: National Endowment for the Arts, 2015.

"DePauw's 21st Century Musician Initiative Is 'Making Classical New'." *DePauw University.* Accessed September 5, 2018. www.depauw.edu/news-media/latest-news/details/31169/.

DeVeaux, S. *Jazz in America: Who's Listening?* Report no. 31. Research Division, National Endowment for the Arts. Carson, CA: Seven Locks Press, 1995.

"Entrepreneurial Coursework at the Juilliard School." *The Juilliard School.* Accessed September 5, 2018. www.juilliard.edu/school/career-services/entrepreneurial-coursework.

"Everyone Listens to Music, But How We Listen Is Changing." *Nielsen*, January 22, 2015. Accessed September 7, 2018. www.nielsen.com/us/en/insights/news/2015/everyone-listens-to-music-but-how-we-listen-is-changing.html.

"Examples of Innovative Ensembles." *Peabody Conservatory*, September, 2017. Accessed September 5, 2018. https://peabody.jhu.edu/wp-content/uploads/2017/09/examples_of_innovative_ensembles.pdf.

Freeman, R. *The Crisis of Classical Music in America: Lessons from a Life in the Education of Musicians.* Lanham, MD: Rowman & Littlefield, 2014.

Goodstein, R., E. Pin, and R. McCurdy. "The New Performing-Arts Curriculum." *Chronicle of Higher Education* 63, no. 7 (October 14, 2017): A24.

Hugill, A. *The Digital Musician* (2nd ed.). New York, NY: Routledge, 2012.

Ivey, B. *Arts, Inc.: How Greed and Neglect Have Destroyed Our Cultural Rights.* Berkeley, CA: University of California Press, 2010.

Kaiser, M. "What Is Wrong with the Arts?" *Huffington Post*, March 14, 2011. Accessed September 4, 2018. www.huffingtonpost.com/michael-kaiser/what-is-wrong-with-the-ar_b_822757.html.

Kingsbury, H. *Music, Talent, and Performance: A Conservatory Cultural System.* Philadelphia: Temple University Press, 2001.

Kozinn, A. "Check the Numbers: Rumors of Classical Music's Demise Are Dead Wrong." *The New York Times*, May 28, 2006. Accessed September 7, 2018. www.nytimes.com/2006/05/28/arts/music/28kozi.html.

La Rosa, D. "Jazz Has Become the Least-Popular Genre in the U.S." *Jazz Line News*, March 9, 2015. Accessed September 7, 2018. https://news.jazzline. com/news/jazz-least-popular-music-genre/.

Lebrecht, N. "Classical Music Isn't Dead, It's Just Too Expensive." *Slipped-Disc*. Accessed September 5, 2018. http://slippedisc.com/2015/01/classical-music-isnt-dead-its-just-too-expensive/

Lopez, S. *Nielsen Music 360 2016 Highlights*. Report. Music, Nielsen. New York, NY: Nielsen Company, 2016.

Lopez, S. *Nielsen Music 360 Report 2015 Highlights*. Report. Music, Nielsen. New York, NY: Nielsen Company, 2015.

Mac Donald, H. "Classical Music's New Golden Age." *City Journal*, January 27, 2016. Accessed September 6, 2018. www.city-journal.org/html/ classical-music's-new-golden-age-13309.html.

Mac Donald, H. "The Unsustainable Declinism of Greg Sandow." *City Journal*, December 23, 2015. Accessed September 6, 2018. www.city-journal. org/html/unsustainable-declinism-greg-sandow-9630.html.

Mantie, R., S. Gulish, G. McCandless, T. Solis, and D. Williams. "Creating Music Curricula of the Future: Preparing Undergraduate Music Students to Engage." *College Music Symposium* 57, (September 27). Accessed September 3, 2018. https://symposium.music.org/index.php?option=com_ k2&view=item&id=11357:creating-music-curricula-of-the-future-preparing-undergraduate-music-students-to-engage&Itemid=124.

McCormick, L. *Performing Civility: International Competitions in Classical Music*. Cambridge: Cambridge University Press, 2015.

McGregor, E.V. *Jazz and Postwar French Identity: Improvising the Nation*. Lanham, MD: Lexington Books, 2016.

Moore, R.D., ed. *College Music Curricula for a New Century*. New York: Oxford University Press, 2017.

Music Consumer Insight Report 2016. Report. Ipsos Connect, International Federation of the Phonographic Industry. London, UK: IFPI, 2017.

Myers, D.E. "New Ideas as Drivers of Curricular Planning and Change: Testing Assumptions; Forging Advances." *Journal of Performing Arts Leadership in Higher Education* 5, (Fall, 2014): 65–77.

Myers, D., E. Sarath, J. Chattah, L. Higgins, V. Levine, D. Rudge, and T. Rice. *Transforming Music Study from Its Foundations: A Manifesto for Progressive Change in the Undergraduate Preparation of Music Majors Report of the Task Force on the Undergraduate Music Major*, College Music Society, November, 2014. Accessed September 2, 2018. www.mtosmt.org/issues/ mto.16.22.1/manifesto.pdf.

News and Notes on 2017 RIAA Revenue Statistics. Accessed September 5, 2018. www.riaa.com/wp-content/uploads/2018/03/RIAA-Year-End-2017-News-and-Notes.pdf.

"Office of Curricular Innovation and Policy." *Admissions: Film and Media Arts: Meadows School of the Arts: SMU*. Accessed September 5, 2018. www.smu.edu/provost/provostoffice/cip.

Panay, P. "Rethinking Music: The Future of Making Money as a Performing Artist." In *Rethinking Music: A Briefing Book*, 57–64. Boston: Berkman

Center for Internet & Society, 2011. Accessed September 4, 2018. https://cyber.harvard.edu/sites/cyber.harvard.edu/files/Rethinking_Music_Briefing_Book_April-25-2011.pdf.

Polisi, J.W. *The Artist as Citizen*. Pompton Plains, NJ: Amadeus Press, 2005.

"Prep/CE Strategic Plan Core Strategies: Curriculum." *New England Conservatory*. Accessed September 5, 2018. https://necmusic.edu/prepce-strategic-plan/curriculum.

Robin, W. "Classical Music Isn't Dead." *New Yorker*, January 29, 2014. Accessed September 5, 2018. www.newyorker.com/culture/culture-desk/the-fat-lady-is-still-singing.

Robin, W. "The Rise and Fall of 'Indie Classical': Tracing a Controversial Term in Twenty-First Century New Music." *Journal of the Society for American Music* 12, no. 1 (February, 2018): 55–88.

Sandow, G. "Cockeyed Optimist." *Arts Journal*, July 25, 2010. Accessed September 6, 2018. www.artsjournal.com/sandow/2010/07/cockeyed_optimist.html.

Sandow, G. "Off in the Clouds." *Arts Journal*, July 27, 2010. Accessed September 6, 2018. www.artsjournal.com/sandow/2010/07/off_in_the_clouds.html.

Sandow, G. "One Last Thought . . . " *Arts Journal*, July 30, 2010. Accessed September 6, 2018. www.artsjournal.com/sandow/2010/07/one_last_thought.html.

Sandow, G. "The Poor Dead Horse." *Arts Journal*, July 30, 2010. Accessed September 6, 2018. www.artsjournal.com/sandow/2010/07/the_poor_dead_horse.html.

Sandow, G. "Still in the Clouds." *Arts Journal*, July 29, 2010. Accessed September 6, 2018. www.artsjournal.com/sandow/2010/07/still_in_the_clouds.html.

Sanjek, R. *American Popular Music and Its Business: The First Four Hundred Years*. New York, NY: Oxford University Press, 1988.

Schoenbach, P.J. "Career Preparation: Moving Into the American Marketplace with the Bachelor of Music in Performance: Innovation and New Thoughts about Performance Training for the Future." *Proceedings, the 75th Annual Meeting, 1999*. Reston, VA: National Association of Schools of Music, 2000: 6–11.

Shuler, S.C. "Music Education for Life: Building Inclusive, Effective Twenty-First Century Music Programs." *Music Educators Journal* 98, no. 1 (09, 2011): 8–13.

Slaughter, J., and D.G. Springer. "What They Didn't Teach Me in My Undergraduate Degree: An Exploratory Study of Graduate Student Musicians' Expressed Opinions of Career Development Opportunities." *College Music Symposium* 55, (October 20, 2015). Accessed September 3, 2018. https://symposium.music.org/index.php?option=com_k2&view=item&id=10889:what-they-didn%E2%80%99t-teach-me-in-my-undergraduate-degree-an-exploratory-study-of-graduate-student-musicians%E2%80%99-expressed-opinions-of-career-development-opportunities.

"Start a Movement." *Admissions: Film and Media Arts: Meadows School of the Arts: SMU*. Accessed September 5, 2018. www.smu.edu/Meadows/TheMovement/ArtsEntrepreneurship.

Stepniak, M. "Beauty, Brilliance, and Expression: On Reimagining Jazz and Classical Music Performance Training & Reconnecting with the General Public." *College Music Symposium* 57, (September 6, 2017). Accessed September 3, 2018. https://symposium.music.org/index.php?option=com_k2&view=item&id=11353:beyond-beauty-brilliance-and-expression-on-reimagining-jazz-and-classical-music-performance-training-reconnecting-with-the-general-public&Itemid=126.

Sturm, J. "Where Do We Go From Here? A Crossroads of Cost and Content for the Arts in Higher Education." *Journal of Performing Arts Leadership in Higher Education* 5, (Fall, 2014): 45–56.

Thompson, D. "Who's to Blame for the Music Industry's Free-Fall?" *The Atlantic*, February 2, 2010. Accessed September 7, 2018. www.theatlantic.com/business/archive/2010/02/whos-to-blame-for-the-music-industrys-free-fall/35212/.

Time with Tunes: How Technology Is Driving Music Consumption. Report. Music, Nielsen. New York, NY: The Nielsen Company, 2017. Accessed September 5, 2018. www.nielsen.com/us/en/insights/news/2017/time-with-tunes-how-technology-is-driving-music-consumption.html.

"The USC Thornton School of Music Announces Five Innovative Master's Degree Programs." *USC Thornton School of Music*. Accessed September 5, 2018. https://music.usc.edu/the-usc-thornton-school-of-music-announces-five-innovative-masters-degree-programs/.

"USC Thornton's Progressive Curriculum Highlighted in the Chronicle of Higher Education." *USC Thornton School of Music*. Accessed September 5, 2018. https://music.usc.edu/usc-thorntons-progressive-curriculum-highlighted-in-the-chronicle-of-higher-education/.

U.S. Sales Database. Report. Sales, Recording Industry Association of America. 2018. Accessed September 5, 2018. www.riaa.com/u-s-sales-database/.

Vanhoenacker, M. "Is Classical Music Dead?" *Slate Magazine*, January 21, 2014. Accessed September 6, 2018. www.slate.com/articles/arts/culturebox/2014/01/classical_music_sales_decline_is_classical_on_death_s_door.html.

Voice, A. "History of the Record Industry, 1920–1950s." *Medium*, June 8, 2014. Accessed September 6, 2018. https://medium.com/@Vinylmint/history-of-the-record-industry-1920-1950s-6d491d7cb606.

Watts, C. "Mixing Things Up: Collaboration, Converging Disciplines, and the Music Curriculum." *Organised Sound* 9, no. 3 (December, 2004): 295–299.

West, M.J. "The New England Conservatory: A Tradition of Innovation." *JazzTimes*. Accessed September 5, 2018. https://jazztimes.com/departments/education/the-new-england-conservatory-a-tradition-of-innovation/.

2 Gathering Insights From the Field

How the Classical Music Marketplace Is Changing, and What That Change Means for the Training That Students Need

Introduction

Observers who are somewhat familiar with the classical music industry may have difficulty understanding why there isn't frenetic and greater curricular innovation and programmatic reorientation within most music schools and conservatories. After all, as the preceding chapter suggests and as most readers of this book will appreciate, the traditional job market for classical musicians has radically changed over the past decades and continues to change even while music performance degrees and preprofessional training offered at many conservatories, colleges, and universities remain significantly unchanged.

A number of higher education music leaders have already shared thoughtful perspective on the general classical music landscape.[1] To further illuminate the types of changes happening within the classical music marketplace and the types of changes that may be needed within classical music performance degree programs, the authors of this book sought insights from a broader array of leaders in the field. Specifically, the authors reached out to solicit insights from a cross section of two types of leaders familiar with classical music training trends and the marketplace: (a) leaders from both public and private and geographically dispersed higher education music units; and (b) a cross section of leaders from music/arts industry organizations, geographically dispersed and of different sizes.

To gather insights from these leaders, the authors used the process of surveying, employing a carefully developed questionnaire to collect primary data. Participants (who are referred to as interviewees below) provided their responses either via email or within the context of a focused interview held through recorded Zoom audio (to allow for more consistent transcription).[2] A list of interviewees who provided responses—is outlined in Table 2.1.

As Table 2.1 shows, interviewees from higher education included senior administrators (Associate Deans, Deans, and a President) as well as faculty who have become prominent within the higher education field in promoting or supporting curricular innovation or change in music. The music/arts industry leaders who were selected and who sent the authors written responses to the questions included not only arts presenters and artist managers but also conductors who have been associated with orchestras that (in terms of budgets and size) represent the more common type of orchestra offering full-season employment in the United States.[28] Of the 25 individuals who ultimately responded and shared responses and insights, seven were female and almost all were Caucasian, in that way representing a field that continues to be dominated by male leaders and populated by few people of color. (More on the issue of lack of gender and racial/ethnic diversity in classical music leadership—and recommended strategies to better address that issue—in chapter 3.)

Interviewees from both higher education and music/arts industry organizations were asked a handful of interrelated questions, as outlined in Table 2.2.

Table 2.1 Interviewees

From *Music Units in Higher Education*	From *Music/Arts Industry Organizations*
Angela Myles Beeching,[3] Arts Career Specialist, Director of the Center for Music Entrepreneurship at Manhattan School of Music, leading author/consultant on career preparation for classical musicians	Jenny Bilfield,[19] President and CEO, Washington Performing Arts
	William "Bill" Capone,[20] Managing Director, Arts Management Group
	Kristy Edmunds,[21] Executive and Artistic Director, Center for the Art of Performance at UCLA
Abra Bush,[4] Senior Associate Dean of Institute Studies, Peabody Institute, Johns Hopkins University	Andrew Lane,[22] Managing Director, Curtis on Tour, Curtis Institute of Music, and former Booking Agent with Opus 3 Artists
Judy Bundra,[5] Dean of the Conservatory and Chief Academic Officer, Cleveland Institute of Music	Stuart Malina,[23] Artistic Director of the Harrisburg Symphony, Principal Guest Conductor of the Florida Orchestra
Fred Bronstein,[6] Dean of the Peabody Institute, Johns Hopkins University	

From *Music Units in Higher Education*	From *Music/Arts Industry Organizations*
Robert Cutietta,[7] Dean of the Thornton School of Music and the Kaufman School of Dance, University of Southern California	André Raphel,[24] Conductor Laureate of the Wheeling Symphony Orchestra, previously Assistant Conductor of the Philadelphia Orchestra and Saint Louis Symphony
David Cutler,[8] Associate Professor, Music Entrepreneurship, School of Music, University of South Carolina	Courtney Reilly,[25] Artistic Director of Performing Arts Live and Managing Director, Shenandoah Conservatory of Shenandoah University
James Doser,[9] Director of the Institute for Music Leadership, Eastman School of Music, University of Rochester	Steve Wogaman,[26] President, Chamber Music Society of Detroit
Robert Freeman,[10] former Dean of the College of Fine Arts and Professor Emeritus of Musicology at Butler School of Music, University of Texas at Austin; former President of the New England Conservatory and Director of the Eastman School of Music, University of Rochester	John Zion,[27] Managing Director, MKI Artists
Richard Goodstein,[11] Dean of Architecture, Arts, and Humanities, Clemson University	
Tayloe Harding,[12] Dean of the School of Music, University of South Carolina	
Paul Hogle,[13] President, Cleveland Institute of Music	
David Myers,[14] Professor of Music Education, College of Liberal Arts, University of Minnesota	
Brian Pertl,[15] Dean of Lawrence Conservatory of Music, Lawrence University	
Mary Ellen Poole,[16] Director of the Butler School of Music, University of Texas at Austin	
Greg Sandow,[17] Professor of Music, Graduate Studies, The Juilliard School, music critic and blogger, composer	
Keith Ward,[18] Director of the Lamont Music School, University of Denver, and President of College Music Society	

Table 2.2 Questions Posed to Interviewees

Insight Sought . . .	Specific Question Asked	
	. . . of Higher Education Leaders	. . . of Music/Arts Industry Leaders
. . . into the most significant changes to classical music audiences and the marketplace.	"If you had to pick just one or two, what do you sense are the most significant changes related to classical music audiences or the entertainment marketplace that will continue to impact the job prospects for our classical music performances students in the years ahead?"	"It's broadly known that audience preferences for classical music programs and classical musical solo artists and ensembles continue to change. What are the two or three most significant ways that you sense audience/listener preferences for classical music programs and artists will continue changing in the coming years?"
. . . into what music schools/ programs should be doing differently to prepare students for success in that changing marketplace.	"If you had to pinpoint just one or two things, what do you think our conservatories and music schools should do differently to better prepare classical music performance students for success in the performing arts marketplace?"	"While conservatories and music schools typically voice a commitment to preparing classical music students for success in the current and future marketplace, it's likely that we could do that work better. If you had to pinpoint just one or two things, what do you think our schools should do differently to better prepare music performance students for success in the performing arts marketplace?"
. . . into skills, competencies, or knowledge that would help classical music	"If there was one piece of advice you could give a young classical musician aspiring to a career as a performer (whether as a soloist or in an ensemble), what would it be?"	"If there was one piece of advice you could give a young classical musician aspiring to a career as a performer (whether as a soloist or in an ensemble), what would it be?"

Insight Sought . . .	Specific Question Asked	
	. . . of Higher Education Leaders	. . . of Music/Arts Industry Leaders
performance students be better positioned for career success in that changing marketplace.		AND *"Assuming that their musicianship is equally strong, are there any qualities or attributes that are likely to help some musical artists be more successful than others in (a) attracting your favorable attention, and (b) enabling you to build ticket sales and audience draw?"*
. . . into how higher education music leaders might best enable significant and swift curricular change.	*"For many good reasons, curricular change in higher education has traditionally required slow and incremental work. A fast-changing performing arts marketplace, however, is demanding we make rapid and large-scale curricular changes to offered degrees. What one piece of advice would you share with the music department chair or music school dean wondering how to help her faculty pursue a big/bold reimagining of music performance curriculum to better prepare graduates for that marketplace and full-time employment?"*	Not asked about this.

To confirm, each interviewee received these questions at the point of initial outreach and invitation to participate in this study, along with an explanation that shared opinions would be used in this monograph. All interviewees who ended up participating confirmed their understanding and agreement that their shared opinions were to be included in this monograph. Each interviewee then had the option to either reply in writing or to share responses during a recorded Zoom audio interview. The majority of higher education interviewees opted to answer the provided questions via a recorded interview, and interviewees from music/arts industry all opted to submit responses to the questions in writing.

This chapter focuses around the issues and insights related to the first three of the questions. The fourth question in this study, pointing as it does to a complex array of issues and concerns, is investigated separately in the final chapter.

Interviewee responses to the first three question sets are described and analyzed in the rest of this chapter, organized by question and including both a summary of responses received by question topic and clarification of themes that became apparent among interviewee responses within each question topic. Following a report of interviewee responses to the first three question sets, this chapter moves to a discussion of the potential implications that gathered insights have for curriculum, specifically as related to needed student learning outcomes in music degrees. It then closes with acknowledgment of the potential alignment of those possible new student-learning outcomes with the core skills and competencies that the business community increasingly affirms are needed for general twenty-first-century careers.

I.   Interviewee Responses Regarding the Most Significant Changes to Classical Music Audiences and Marketplace

Both higher education leaders and presenters/agents/conductors were asked about changes that would impact job prospects for future classical music performers. Their precise questions are again reproduced here.

> Educators were asked: "If you had to pick just one or two, what do you sense are the most significant changes related to classical music audiences or the entertainment marketplace that will continue

Table 2.3 Most Mentioned Factors or Issue Areas in Responses to Question
Regarding *Most Significant Changes to Classical Music Audiences
and Marketplace*

Factor/Issue Area Mentioned	Number of Mentions
Increased audience preference for authentic engagement/connection or for new experiences	20 mentions
Changing demographics in society, and emerging new tastes/priorities	9 mentions
Factors antagonistic to traditional classical music concerts and listening	6 mentions
Presence of disruptive technology	5 mentions
Audience's decreasing familiarity with (and interest in) classical music	5 mentions

to impact the job prospects for our classical music performances students in the years ahead?"

Presenters, artist managers, and conductors were asked: "It's broadly known that audience preferences for classical music programs and classical musical solo artists and ensembles continue to change. What are the two or three most significant ways that you sense audience/listener preferences for classical music programs and artists will continue changing in the coming years?"

Interviewees ended up pointing to multiple areas of changes. A close investigation revealed, however, that several issue areas were referenced with special frequency by individuals in both organization types. Those issue areas (sorted by frequency of mention), are summarized in Table 2.3 and then described in further detail thereafter.

1. Increased Audience Preference for Authentic Engagement/Connection or for New Experiences

The issue/area most commonly raised by interviewees was that of the strong (and ongoing) preference among audiences for experiences that differ from the previously traditional concert, because they offer audiences either a more authentically engaging experience or a very new experience.

The issue of authentic engagement or connection came up frequently. The descriptions of that desire for engagement or connection were multiple, including the following:

> "people want to connect" (faculty leader David Cutler); "audiences want to connect with performing musicians more" (director Keith Ward); "audiences crave engagement" (presenter Steve Wogaman); "audiences and donors . . . crave a more personal, more authentic relationship" (president Paul Hogle); "both artists and audiences are increasingly compelled toward intimacy" (presenter Kristy Edmunds); "audiences will want to engage with artists in new ways" (presenter Courtney Reilly);

Along similar lines, a number of interviewees made a point of differentiating traditional concerts from experiences, implying that the traditional concert was a passive event, whereas what audiences wanted was an experience that enabled them to connect and engage. For example, faculty leader David Cutler pointed out that audiences had an "increasing desire for experiences over concerts." Artist manager Andrew Lane argued that audiences will continue having preference "for interesting educational concert experiences." And director Keith Ward explained that "audiences seek less to go to concerts . . . and more to events." While most interviewees did not expound on the types of factors that made the imagined performance programming more of an event than a concert, some did add clarification. Artist manager Lane, for example, explained that changes in audience preferences for the types of experiences described above had "less to do with genres . . . and more to do with concert format and audience engagement."

Interestingly, there was mention of audience hunger for truly novel repertoire or experimentation— "interest in smaller diverse ensembles" (dean Rob Cutietta); collaboration across genres (presenter Kristy Edmunds); "performances that incorporate multi-disciplinary performing arts" (artist manager Lane); the continued growth of "Interest in world music . . . of film music and programs that combine various art forms such as music and dance" (conductor André Raphel). Some respondents also took care to clarify that audience hunger for new experiences was far from universal across the country. As dean Rob Cutietta explained, the "real eagerness" that he witnessed in Los Angeles for "new things, experimental things" was not present in many other places in the country; the openness and interest in novel and experimental experiences was different in "middle America vs LA." Conductor Stuart Malina put it succinctly: audience tastes and preferences "differ from place to place and from demographic to demographic."

2. Changing Demographics in Society, and Emerging New Tastes/Priorities

The second-most mentioned issue was one related to changing society demographics and new tastes and priorities. As respondents explained, there will be ongoing "demand for a great diversity of voices in classical music programming (presenter Courtney Reilly), and there will be a "push to highlight music by racially diverse and/or female composers" (artist manager John Zion). Director Mary Ellen Poole pointed to the "evolution of donor priorities," with their ongoing likelihood to continue targeting "their philanthropy at social justice, environment . . . rather than legacy arts . . . who themselves may appear to be slow to evolve." And several respondents linked changing tastes and priorities not only to changing demographics but also to the increased entertainment options audiences face. As director Keith Ward explained, it is a "crowded marketplace," and Dean Tayloe Harding spoke of "such a diverse plethora of music styles that they [i.e., audiences] can choose from."

3. Factors Antagonistic to Traditional Classical Music Concerts and Listening

Perhaps not surprisingly, one of the most frequently mentioned issues was aspects of culture and society that were antagonistic to the understanding and appreciation of traditional classical music listening. Director Jim Doser referenced audiences' increased "unwillingness to sit for short or longer time," and senior associate dean Abra Bush spoke of the "culture of immediate gratification." Presenter Jenny Bilfield went further, explaining that we are "at an existential crossroads in making a case for live music, period." Several respondents took aim squarely at the damage that classical musicians and music has done to its own reputation and quality. As dean Brian Pertl explained, "classical music performances are seen as elitist, snooty affairs . . . lack diversity . . . not welcoming to all audiences." Arts leader Greg Sandow put it even more simply: "audiences are tired of the arts self-interested industry."

4. *Presence of Disruptive Technology and Audience's Decreasing Familiarity With (and Interest in) Classical Music*

There were five mentions among respondents of disruptive technology, including media platforms that hooked attention. In describing what was increasingly attracting audience attention, respondents spoke to the range of "delivery systems" (senior associate dean Abra Bush), or "technology" (dean Fred Bronstein); "social media" (dean Judy Bundra); and "technology, websites, digital recordings" (dean Tayloe Harding). And respondents also made five mentions of the decreasing familiarity with and interest in classical music. Dean Fred Bronstein spoke of "lost generations of music education in schools." Director Mary Ellen Poole explained that "the quantitative assessment obsession in primary and secondary education . . . erosion of support for arts in our schools . . . will populate our audience and donor base with less emotionally and intellectually connected patrons." One respondent, presenter Kristy Edmunds, explained that it was "not that classical music preferences are changing [among classical music audiences] . . . but rather largely staying the same or diminishing." Artist manager Bill Capone was alone among all interviewees in dissenting, explaining that "[I] don't think that preferences are changing as much . . . [as many] would like us to believe."

5. *Other*

Beyond making reference to one or more of the issues just discussed, a couple of respondents also pointed to other changes/issue areas. Dean Judy Bundra pointed to the economics/job availability issue, explaining that the economic instability facing current musicians means they won't retire, and it will be "extra difficult for new/emerging [musicians] to move into those positions." Dean Richard Goodstein explained it was a "simple matter of supply and demand. Too many qualified candidates [for the full-time jobs available in classical music organizations]."

II. Interviewee Responses Regarding What Music Schools/Programs Should Be Doing Differently to Better Prepare Students for Success in That Changing Marketplace

Both higher education leaders and presenters/agents/conductors were asked what schools should do differently to better prepare classical music performance students for success in the performing arts marketplace. The two questions are reproduced here:

Table 2.4 Mentioned Factors or Issue Areas in Responses to Question
Regarding *What's Needed to Better Prepare Students for Success
in the Performing Arts Marketplace?*

Factor/Issue Area Mentioned	Number of Mentions
Train musicians who can better advocate and newly package/present experiences around classical music	20 mentions
Train musicians to figure out/adapt to the new marketplace (with its multiple and changing career options) and shape that marketplace anew	12 mentions
Train musicians with stronger business skills and acumen	6 mentions
Train musicians with new and different music skills and products	4 mentions
Train musicians to employ technology more strategically	1 mention
Train musicians who have competencies in most of these areas	5 mentions

Educators were asked: "If you had to pinpoint just one or two things, what do you think our conservatories and music schools should do differently to better prepare classical music performance students for success in the performing arts marketplace?"

Presenters, artist managers, and conductors were asked: "While Conservatories & Music Schools typically voice a commitment to preparing classical music students for success in the current and future marketplace, it's likely that we could do that work better. If you had to pinpoint just one or two things, what do you think our schools should do differently to better prepare music performance students for success in the performing arts marketplace?"

In their written and verbal responses, interviewees referenced multiple areas of needed change. A close investigation of responses, pursued with an eye to illuminating core themes, revealed the following reasons (listed by number of mentions) (see Table 2.4).

1.　*Train Musicians Who Can Better Advocate and Newly Package/Present Experiences Around Classical Music*

The change most often mentioned by interviewees when asked what changes were needed in schools and programs to better support student career success in the changed marketplace was to train students who could go far beyond the traditional role of performer and better advocate for and newly package and present experiences around classical music performance.

Repeatedly, interviewees made reference to the importance of teaching students to be more appropriately oriented toward the actual job market, specifically by becoming effective advocates for their music. Examples follow: schools and programs should do better in creating "instructional experiences for community engagement" (dean Tayloe Harding); should "educate students as change agents—who can experiment and pilot new concerts" (faculty leader David Myers); should "blow up traditional recital/jury/concert so that students would have to design" (senior associate dean Abra Bush); and should help students be content creators; there will always be someone who plays better (dean Rob Cutietta). Summarizing the need to engage more strategically and aggressively, director Mary Ellen Poole explained that schools needed to "help students understand that concert music no longer has the luxury of pretending to be above the fray—and help them practice addressing this."

Many of the interviewees went further in specifying how students might learn how to better advocate and newly package/present their art. Quite a few interviewees spoke of the importance of strengthening student communication skills. Schools and programs, interviewees explained, should do better in training emerging musicians who have "broader skills in communication" (dean Fred Bronstein); who "are flexible and engaging in front of audiences" and "can write well" (senior associate dean Abra Bush); and who know how "to read, write, think, speak" (dean Robert Freeman). Conductor Stuart Malina shared that "it will be more important for these musicians to know how to speak to audiences, both from the stage and person to person." As presenter Courtney Reilly explained, it is "even more important for institutions to prepare music students to connect with audiences on a human level—to be able to communicate about their craft and why it's relevant and important today." Artist manager Bill Capone went further, explaining that "this is a people business . . . those who have the ability to relate well with people and varying situations will often succeed where those who may have better artistic and technical skills but no skills in relating to other people . . . do not [succeed]." And artist manager John Zion, highlighting the importance of graduating students who have integrity and the ability to make and keep positive interpersonal connections, advised that "it is imperative that a young musician, while still in school, starts to develop a reputation as a compelling performer, a reliable partner, and a person of great integrity."

2. Train Musicians to Figure Out/Adapt to the New Marketplace (With Its Multiple and Changing Career Options) and Shape That Marketplace Anew

The third most mentioned recommendation by interviewees related to giving students greater ownership or control of their education and allowing them to shape a career using their own smarts. Dean Rob Cutietta explained that schools need to do better in having "classical kids take control of their education." He continued by remarking on the difference he saw between students engaged in popular music study, and those focused on classical music performance.

> [It's] really interesting how different students are in these fields. . . . Contemporary—hungry, [asking] "how can I change my world with music, how do I get my music in front of people." Classical—very inward looking, playing music for themselves, [hoping that] someone will pay them.

Dean Robert Freeman advised that schools should change to operate with the understanding that students won't have "traditional jobs but jobs that students will invent themselves." Director Jim Doser shared that schools and programs need to "give students permission to define their own definition of success in their lives and discipline," explaining that those schools and programs could better "create space in the current lives of our students to explore connections and have a role in what they study; we could be resource providers." Artist manager Bill Capone put it differently, explaining the benefits of allowing students to personally navigate myriad changes in the marketplace—"the ability to be flexible and versatile gives them more of chance of success." And conductor André Raphel shared that "in addition to being complete musicians, the demand for innovators in the classical field has never been higher." He went on to explain that "presenters and organizations increasingly look to performers to bring innovative ideas, to bridge the gap between a general lack of public attention given to classical music and education."

Many interviewees went further and recommended that schools and programs take a more active role in helping students better understand and be aware of career options and pathways. As dean Judy Bundra explained, students "need to learn about multiple ways to create a meaningful career." Director Keith Ward advised that schools needed to do better to "support students' explorations of building careers in music not limited to performance . . . there is important work to be done in education/engagement, marketing, development, the virtual world, arts administration, and other areas that support music performance." Presenter Jenny Bilfield recommended that schools should "invest in internships where classical music students use their performance other musical skills in new situations: curating a concert, teaching students, marketing a series." And presenter Steve Wogaman took the advice of career flexibility still further, explaining that "with scores of less-satisfied musical graduates as negative examples, I have come to believe that the music curriculum needs a major overhaul, such that it becomes possible with the span of a reasonably-paced four-year bachelor's degree to complete two majors or degrees, of which only one is in music."

3.   Train Musicians With Stronger Business Skills and Acumen

The fourth most mentioned area of change that was mentioned by interviewees was that schools and programs should ensure that students graduate with stronger business skills and acumen. As artist manager John Zion explained, schools and programs should "make sure that students are equipped with strong business and financial skills." Conductor Stuart Malina advised that "it will be more and more important for young musicians to understand entrepreneurship, everything from budgeting to attracting sponsorships, from advertising to hiring personnel." In describing the broader skills that graduating classical musicians now needed, dean Fred Bronstein highlighted the importance of their being trained in "entrepreneurship," and dean Richard Goodstein recommended "classes in marketing, the business of music and entrepreneurship." Presenter Kristy Edmunds summed up this general area of concern by noting that "if the market-factor remains primary for various reasons then ensuring that music students have high-level access to courses in business and economics would seem prudent at a very practical level."

4.   Train Musicians With New and Different Music Skills and Products

Among interviewee responses, there were four mentions of the need to help students graduate with a greater set of musical skills and products. For example, senior associate dean Abra Bush highlighted the importance of graduating students who "can improvise." Consultant Angela Myles Beeching likewise highlighted the importance of teaching students 'improvisation, including theatre improv" to help with communication and interpersonal skills. And director Mary Ellen Poole spoke of the need for schools to "find ways to encourage greater stylistic versatility and flexibility" in student performance.

5. Train Musicians to Employ Technology More Strategically

Interestingly, only one interviewee responded to this core question by highlighting a need for more/different training around technology. Senior associate dean Abra Bush explained that schools needed to do better in helping students understand "how technology can and does impact their music making and career viability."

6. Train Musicians Who Have Competencies in Most of These Areas

A handful of interviewees went beyond highlighting one or two specific recommendations and provided a long list of changes needed. For example, president Paul Hogle outlined the extraordinary range of knowledge, skills, and attributes that schools needed to better inculcate:

> beyond preparation in the studio . . . preparation has to be for their ability to be successful in a career . . . trying to talk about the learning they would need, regardless of their career. Everything from managing anxiety, to marketing/fundraising, to nonprofit law, to labor relations, to use of music as a weapon in community building and equity/diversity/inclusion.

Senior associate dean Abra Bush likewise outlined a vision of a super-musician/advocate, explaining that

> The best thing we can do to prepare classical music performance students for success is to make sure that they are not only well prepared technically on their instrument, but have more than a fundamental understanding of how technology can and does impact their music making, and career viability; they are flexible, adaptable and engaging in front of audiences; they can improve; they can write well; and they are good colleagues . . . students need to learn about multiple ways to create a meaningful career.

And, making reference to the importance of graduating musicians who were as virtuosic as performers and programmers as they were effective advocates and communicators and negotiators, dean Tayloe Harding advised that,

> in addition to preparing young people to be best musicians they can be, [schools] help them become the best sales people— understanding a community's needs, how talent aligns with community's needs. . . . Music schools should prepare a holistic musician that is different . . . we're talking about preparing musical leaders . . . music leaders identify a need for music in their community (whatever that nee is, wherever it is—community center, elementary schools, etc.), and find a way to deliver that— determines the music needs and uses their skills to bring to bear on that community's needs.

III.   Interviewee Responses Regarding How Classical Music Performance Students Might Be Better Positioned for Career Success

Both higher education leaders and presenters/agents/conductors were asked to illuminate ways that students could be better prepared for success in the marketplace.

> Educators were asked: "If there was one piece of advice you could give a young classical musician aspiring to a career as a performer (whether as a soloist or in an ensemble), what would it be?"
>
> Presenters, artist managers, and conductors were asked two questions: "If there was one piece of advice you could give a young classical musician aspiring to a career as a performer (whether as a soloist or in an ensemble), what would it be?"
> AND
> "Assuming that their musicianship is equally strong, are there any qualities or attributes that are likely to help some musical artists be more successful than others in (attracting your favorable attention, and (b) enabling you to build ticket sales and audience draw?"

To be clear, these questions (and interviewee responses to same) reveal insights that are relevant not only to students but also to faculty and higher education leaders, illuminating how curricula might be further changed to support the career success of graduating students.

The interviewees ended up pointing to multiple aspects of the change referenced in the question posed. A close investigation of their

Table 2.5 Most Mentioned Factors or Issue Areas in responses to Question Regarding *How Classical Music Performance Students Can Be Better Positioned for Career Success*

Factor/Issue Area Mentioned	Number of Mentions
Have openness/curiosity	12 mentions
Be authentic and take ownership	9 mentions
Build bridges/relationships	8 mentions
Have broad skills and also nontraditional skills	8 mentions

responses revealed the following hierarchy (by number of mentions) (see Table 2.5).

1. Have Openness/Curiosity

Repeatedly, interviewees pointed to the value and need for musicians to be open and curious. Examples of quotes are reproduced here.

"The other thing I always tell [students]; be open to where life takes you! You can't imagine what tomorrow might bring" (dean Fred Bronstein); "remain open to a performing career which may not resemble that of your friends or teachers" (senior associate dean Abra Bush); "don't self-limit your education curiosity . . . take advantage of visiting artists with life insights that can illuminate . . . be a model of curiosity and exploration" (president Paul Hogle)

Presenter Jenny Bilfield advised students to not only "commit to excellence, but also retain your curiosity" and explained her attraction as a presenter to "musicians who are curious and engaged in the world around them." Presenter Courtney Reilly likewise spoke of being "attracted to musicians who are flexible and inventive. . . . I love artists who are curious about the world around them, the communities they are visiting, and the audiences they are engaging." Dean Judy Bundra advised students to "be flexible and willing to learn—be open to new opportunities for you never know where they will lead." Along similar lines, conductor Stuart Malina shared that students should "be as flexible as possible, both stylistically and musically," and conductor André Raphel likewise spoke of the importance of students' ability to understand "varying styles and be flexible. Be ready for a career in which you will play classical, Broadway, jazz, opera, ballet and other genres." As he went on to explain, "those who succeed are constantly stretching the boundaries trying new approaches to presenting concerts and carving out unique niches for themselves as artists."

2.   Be Authentic and Take Ownership

Educators and agents/conductors likewise highlighted the need for classical music performers to take ownership of their career goal and to be authentic. Examples of quotes are reproduced.

> "perform the music that *you* love, make music with people you respect and admire" (senior associate dean Abra Bush); "stop worshipping your professors, see them as your colleagues and demand to have an equal say in your education" (dean Rob Cutietta); "tell them [the students] to follow their hearts" (arts leader Greg Sandow); "The advice I always give [students] is 'absolutely pursue your dream—[but] make sure it's *your* dream'" (dean Fred Bronstein)

A number of presenters likewise spoke of the attractiveness of musicians who, as Edmunds put it, "have a compelling story behind their work". Artist manager Andrew Lane shared that the musicians who stood out for him were artists who "have a unique and compelling platform; what they stand for, what they care deeply about, the kind of music that speaks to them, or what they spend their time doing outside of performing." Presenter Courtney Reilly explained that "artists who have a clear vision of who they are, what they value, and why they are in the room are able to convey that to audiences in a way that is authentic and true."

3.   Build Bridges/Relationships and Have Broad Skills and Also Nontraditional Skills

The third most-mentioned recommendation or area of skill highlighted by interviewees related to the ability of classical music performers to build bridges and relationships and the importance of them having broad and nontraditional skills.

The reasons for the recommendations regarding building bridges and relationships, as the illustrative quotations show, ranged from the philosophical to the practical. "Never bad-mouth a colleague," conductor Stuart Malina advised; "be the kind of person that others want to be around and work with." Artist manager Andrew Lane shared that "it's all about relationships. Go out of your way to build positive relationships everywhere you go. This is a small industry that we work in." Along the same lines, dean Judy Bundra explained that her first recommendation to students was "to be kind—it's a small world and everyone knows everyone." Artist manager Bill Capone referenced the practical side of the performer-agent/presenter relationship when explaining that "it is almost as important to get them [agents/presenters] to like you [the artist] as a person as it is to have them like your performance . . . the artist needs the presenter more than the presenter needs him or her." Along similar lines, conductor André Raphel explained that "the persona and ability of artists to communicate outside the musical community is vital. . . . Those performers who can help bridge the gap not only as important voices for the music, but also as spokespeople about what the arts bring to the community attract more attention."

Interviewees also highlighted the importance of students and classical music performers building broader and nontraditional skills. Examples of those recommendations are outlined here.

Dean Fred Bronstein explained that "your ability to be successful (even in an orchestra) includes your ability to do all sorts of things outside of performance [and] kinds of music performed." Faculty leader Myers gave examples of the breadth of knowledge and range of skills students should develop: "get yourself some good coursework and experience in teaching (classroom as well as individual studio) get experience in arts other than music . . . need some business knowledge . . . learn to engage audiences." Presenter Jenny Bilfield spoke of how musicians with broad skill sets were attractive to presenters/agents when she highlighted the attractiveness of those musicians "who are comfortable engaging with a wider audience through social media and creative collaborations." Conductor André Raphel explained that the artists who are likely to be of greatest interest are those who "are looking beyond the standard repertoire, to large scale projects such as commissions, presentations with video components and cross collaborations with other artists."

Along similar lines, presenter Kristy Edmunds spoke of the attractiveness of those musicians who are "willing and able to co-promote one's work through their own independent channels." Artist manager Lane pointed to the same concern when he explained that "promoting an artist's platform and materials through a robust online presence including an excellent website and social media presence is equally important in helping an artist stand out." Presenter Steve Wogaman put the need for expanded skills beyond performance into further perspective when explaining that "gone are the days when the good word of a well-established manager is enough to sell either presenters or their audiences on an unfamiliar artist." Critical now, Wogaman went on to explain, are things such as "a compelling website (ideally with live, unedited performance videos available on YouTube) as well as great photography."

4. *Other*

Beyond the responses and recommendations highlighted here, interviewees also offered additional and unique suggestions and insights in response to the questions. Two spoke to the importance of perseverance. Conductor Stuart Malina advised students not only to "work really hard . . . the field gets more and more talented year after year, so you'd better be really amazing" but also to "always be impeccably prepared." And artist manager Bill Capone advised students of the importance of "Patience . . . this is a marathon and not a sprint for most artists and groups." He went on to offer an example, sharing that "Mitsuko Uchida came in 2nd in the Warsaw Chopin Competition behind Garrick Ohlsson in 1970. She did not make her Carnegie debut until 1991. You do not know when opportunities will present themselves but you must be ready for them when they do."

Two interviewees made reference to the importance of visual image. Reflecting on what makes some musicians stand out to presenters and agents, presenter Kristy Edmunds reflected that classical music performers should "make friends with great photographers and videographers—a CD of your music is not enough no matter how brilliantly recorded and awesome it is." Along similar lines, conductor Stuart Malina reflected that "sadly, but certainly, good looks, great photos, and youth all help bring in audiences."[29]

One interviewee advised that it is critically important for students to take time to deliberately unplug and to spend time each week away from the hyperconnection enabled through technology. Consultant Angela Myles Beeching recommended strongly that for at least one hour per week, students "unplug, and go by themselves somewhere in nature to reflect; to process," explaining that being so unplugged "creates a learning that is otherwise not possible." (Interestingly, she reflected that she used to think one hour per day was appropriate but that she now realizes that it is likely difficult for current students to do even as much as one hour per week.)

Finally, one interviewee reflected on a comprehensive strategy that students should pursue in better preparing for a successful career. Sharing a number of specific actions, artist manager John Zion advised students to follow "a three step plan" which would help a student to "clarify your artistic vision . . . develop a strategic plan to achieve that vision . . . [and] convert these artistic ideals into a product that will sell in the market."

Reflection

As the overview of interviewee responses reveals, leaders in higher education and music industry fields understand that there are many significant changes that have occurred and are occurring in classical music audiences and the classical music marketplace. Responses revealed that those leaders believe there are a number of things that our higher education institutions should do better prepare students for careers within that changing marketplace.

Table 2.6 provides an overview of the findings outlined in the preceding sections, summarizing the insights provided by the interviewees as sorted by theme and frequency of mention.

The insights shared by interviewees have many implications. To further investigate those implications, the next section begins with general observations regarding the insights shared by interviewees in response to the first question listed in the chart above (and emerging themes within same). It then moves to consider the potential implications of all the responses analyzed here for music training, specifically for degree-level student learning outcomes that might be newly appropriate. The chapter then closes with a reflection on an additional curiosity, the potential alignment between the type of reoriented training that appears to be needed for our students (given what interviewees have affirmed are the needs of the marketplace), and the core skills that appear to be necessary for success in general twenty-first-century careers.

Table 2.6 Interviewee Responses by Frequency of Mention

ISSUE: Most significant changes to classical music audiences and the marketplace?	ISSUE: What should music schools/programs be doing differently to prepare students for success in that changing marketplace?	ISSUE: What skills, competencies, and/or knowledge would help emerging classical music performers/students be better positioned for career success in that changing marketplace?
1. Increased audience preference for authentic engagement/ connection, and/or for new experiences (20 mentions)	1. Train musicians who can better advocate and newly package/ present experiences around classical music (20 mentions)	1. Have openness/ curiosity (12 mentions)
2. Changing demographics, and emerging new tastes/priorities (9 mentions)	2. Train musicians to figure out/adapt to the new marketplace (with its multiple and changing career options) and shape that marketplace anew (12 mentions)	2. Be authentic and take ownership (9 mentions)
3. Legacy of factors antagonistic to traditional classical music concerts and listening (6 mentions)	3. Train musicians with stronger business skills and acumen (6 mentions)	3. Build bridges/ relationships AND Have broad skills and non-traditional skills. (Both 8 mentions)
4. Presence of disruptive technology. AND Audience's decreasing familiarity with and interest in classical music. (Both 5 mentions)	4. Train musicians with new and different musical skills and products (4 mentions)	4. Other a. Perseverance (2) b. Good visual images (2) c. Ability to unplug (1) d. Strategic career plan (1)
5. Other: economics/ job availability; job market supply and demand. (Both 1 mention)	5. Train musicians to employ technology more strategically (1 mention)	
	6. Train musicians who have competencies in most of these areas (5 mentions)	

General Observations on Responses to the Question
Regarding Changing Audiences and Marketplace

Most readers will likely be unsurprised by the insights that interviewees offered regarding changes to classical music audiences and the related marketplace. Interviewees strongly affirmed audiences' growing interest in more engaging experiences, spoke of demographically based changes in tastes, and often referred to a major shift (amid growing range of possible experiences) of audiences embracing new and engaging experiences.[30] Not surprisingly, some interviewees who engage in fundraising as part of their professional activities pointed out the shift in donor preferences away from supporting such causes as "legacy" arts organizations toward supporting causes typically more closely aligned with human welfare (environmental and social justice causes), a well-documented trend.[31]

Perhaps one of the findings that might strike readers as particularly surprising is that there isn't more agreement among leaders regarding which issues and changes in the marketplace are truly *most* significant, and that there wasn't more mention of disruptive technology (an often-mentioned issue).[32] That lack of uniform agreement is understandable. In the midst of a changing landscape, where almost every single aspect of that change is sizable and disruptive, it should be of little surprise that there is a lack of agreement regarding which changes are most significant. Consider: even if only one of the least mentioned factors were true, that factor alone would severely challenge education and training models. Given that *all* of the issues/changes might be fairly described as significant (and many more besides!), it may be little wonder that there is difficulty in briefly and succinctly describing what stood out and was most significant. Perhaps even more important, the current changes in the classical music performance industry marketplace may be so multifaceted and the range of actions needed to realign preparation with that changed marketplace so varied and multiple that there may well be a shared inability to truly grasp the scope and content of the issue/problem.

Put in different terms, the problem is not only complicated, it is *complex*. Unlike complicated problems that are hard but can be solved (e.g., getting an astronaut to the moon and back), the multifaceted issues related to classical music's decline in society and higher education's potential role in addressing same is (like the problem of raising a teenager) of a type that author Rick Nason has called a complex problem—a problem or situation that involves too many unknowns and too many interrelated factors to lend itself to any solution.[33]

Readers may also find it surprising that interviewee responses included little reference to any analysis of economic and cultural trends. But it might be possible that shared insights built more on interviewees' idiosyncratic professional experiences than on shared examination and understanding of such trends. If true, it would certainly be understandable; leaders in higher education and the arts face an extraordinary range of immediate concerns leaving little time and energy for a meaningful analysis of macro-economic and society-wide changes.

Potential Implications for Curriculum, as It Relates to Student Learning Outcomes in Music Degrees

There are many ways to consider the implications of the insights shared by these higher education and music/arts industry professionals. What would it mean if we were to take *all* the insights shared to heart and shape a music performance curriculum that is indeed aligned with these insights?[34] One of the most helpful ways to consider the implications of shared insights when it comes to curriculum is in terms of something increasingly stressed by accrediting associations and familiar to higher education faculty; namely, degree-level student learning outcomes.

Student learning outcomes—what Peter Ewell defined in his seminal 2001 work as "the particular levels of knowledge, skills, and abilities that a student has attained at the end (or as a result) of his or her engagement in a particular set of collegiate experiences"[35]—are highly useful here for two reasons. First, most music faculty are highly familiar with the concept of degree-level student learning outcomes. Second, student learning outcomes provide clarity and focus regarding the orientation of a degree without predetermining how each supporting curricular and cocurricular element within that degree will be shaped. Different campuses and programs, that is to say, can create very different curriculum maps in support of the same student learning outcomes.

If we were to take seriously the insights shared and described by interviewees, we would certainly be reshaping our degree-level student learning outcomes and creating ones that are very different from those typically found at our institutions. As the two illustrative examples show—both taken from 2018–2019 program descriptions—the student learning outcomes typically found in our Bachelor of Music degrees privilege academic knowledge and technical competencies appropriate for the type of career preparation that has not been relevant since the mid-twentieth century: preparing our students for auditions held by traditional ensembles (orchestras or opera companies) and for participation in competitions. (Notice that the lists presented in Table 2.7, pulled from websites at the respective institutions, include no mention of such central skills as those related to engaging and connecting with and building audiences, possession of business skills, or knowledge and competencies around technology or marketing.)

It is important to note that *not one* of the interviewees in this study asserted that students should be less skilled on their instruments or have a musicianship that is far less informed by historical or theoretical knowledge. What their comments revealed, rather, was the urgent need we in the academy face to help our graduates develop an additional and different set of competencies and knowledge areas given the changed classical music marketplace.

If we were to take these insights of higher education and music/arts industry leaders seriously, how might we imagine those student learning outcomes? Table 2.8 lists again the core themes that emerged from an analysis of the shared insights by these higher education and music/arts industry leaders.

There are many ways to envision a set of student learning outcomes that would bring music training within a degree program like the general Bachelor of Music degree into alignment with the above realities. One possible list of student learning outcomes is outlined immediately below Table 2.8. (To be clear, this is one of many such possible lists, and is included here primarily to spur thinking.) As the reader might immediately perceive, the student learning outcomes outlined therein have great implication for much of the core curriculum; they would likely require that most current core courses (whether studio lessons, ensembles, juries, or courses in music theory and history) be significantly tweaked or reimagined from their current focus.

Table 2.7 Typical Student Learning Outcomes for Undergraduate Music Degrees: Two Current and Illustrative Examples

BOSTON UNIVERSITY, College of Fine Arts, Bachelor of Music in Performance[36]	WARTBURG COLLEGE, Departments and Programs, Music[37]
Learning Outcomes All students graduating with a **Bachelor of Music** degree are expected to demonstrate: • A practical knowledge of basic music theory, musicianship, and analytical skills. • An appropriate level of technical and interpretive performance skills. • A broad knowledge of music history and associated repertoires of music. • An appropriate level of pedagogical skills. • The ability to apply creative approaches to problem-solving and self-directed study. Students graduating with a **Bachelor of Music in Performance** are *additionally* expected to: • Demonstrate evidence of an advanced level of technical proficiency and artistic judgment on their chosen instrument/voice, through a variety of solo, chamber music, large instrumental/choral ensemble, and operatic performances, as appropriate, over the course of their undergraduate career.	**Intended Student Learning Outcomes** *Students will:* • Integrate the elements of music (music theory, aural skills, and music history) in performance and oral/written expression. • Exhibit advanced performance skills in juried or public performances (through solo, chamber, and/or large ensembles). • Express the value of music in education and a globally defined society via advocacy according to professional ethical guidelines. Additional Intended Student Learning Outcomes by Degree or Concentration *Students will:* • Integrate theoretical and historical knowledge or the liturgy and demonstrate practical skills in a church music setting *(Bachelor of Arts, Church Music concentration).* • Manage professional competencies in piano pedagogy and studio operations required for certification by Music Teachers National Association *(Bachelor of Arts, Piano Pedagogy concentration).* • Demonstrate applied and analytical skills intended to facilitate entrance into a graduate studies program or as independent studio instructors and/or performers *(Bachelor of Music).* • Integrate skills and knowledge for the purpose of effectively teaching music to K-12 students in the public schools in compliance with the standards as established by the Iowa Department of Education *(Bachelor of Music Education; Music Therapy B.M.E.).* • Manage professional competencies in areas of music skills, clinical foundations, and professional behavior required by the American Music Therapy Association *(Music Therapy, B.M. and B.M.E.).*

Table 2.8 Summary of Core Themes and Responses to Key Questions

QUESTION: Most significant changes to classical music audiences and the marketplace?	QUESTION: What should music schools/ programs be doing differently to prepare students for success in that changing marketplace?	QUESTION: What skills, competencies, and/or knowledge would help emerging classical music performers/students be better positioned for career success in that changing marketplace?
1. Increased audience preference for authentic engagement/ connection, and/or for new experiences (20 mentions) 2. Changing demographics and emerging new tastes/ priorities (9 mentions) 3. Legacy of factors antagonistic to traditional classical music concerts and listening (6 mentions) 4. Presence of disruptive technology. AND Audience's decreasing familiarity with and interest in classical music. (Both 5 mentions) 5. Other: economics/job availability; job market supply and demand. (Both 1 mention)	1. Train musicians who can better advocate and newly package/ present experiences around classical music (20 mentions) 2. Train musicians to figure out/ adapt to the new marketplace (with its multiple and changing career options) and shape that marketplace anew (12 mentions) 3. Train musicians with stronger business skills and acumen (6 mentions) 4. Train musicians with new and different musical skills and products (4 mentions) 5. Train musicians to employ technology more strategically (1 mention) 6. Train musicians who have competencies in most of these areas (5 mentions)	1. Have openness/ curiosity (12 mentions) 2. Be authentic and take ownership (9 mentions) 3. Build bridges/ relationships. AND Have broad skills and nontraditional skills. (Both 8 mentions) 4. Other a. Perseverance (2) b. Good visual images (2) c. Ability to unplug (1) d. Strategic career plan (1)

A List of Student Learning Outcomes That Might Better Support Student Success Within the Current Classical Music Marketplace and Music Industry

"All students graduating with a Bachelor of Music in Performance degree are expected to demonstrate:

1.   An ability to engage and connect with general public audiences during performance programs through a technically skilled and personal musical voice, and through verbal communication.
2.   A knowledge of ways musicians (in different settings, genres, and time periods) have engaged and connected with audiences.
3.   A knowledge of the changing classical music marketplace, including knowledge of changes in the tastes and preferences of classical music audiences.
4.   The possession of a personal vision for their music career that builds on a deep awareness of personal skills and broad knowledge of their career opportunities.
5.   An appropriate level of skill in employing social and digital media, including digital music technology, to build audiences and listenership.
6.   The ability to employ appropriate marketing skills and knowledge of online platforms to create a brand and/or product that effectively captures public attention and enables them to stand out in a crowded field of music performers.
7.   An ability to employ a range of business skills that enable them to be successful in managing their finances."

As mentioned earlier, there are multiple ways that this list might be shaped. Readers who object to the order of the skills and competencies listed here should feel assured that the purpose here is not to specify the exact order or length of any list of student learning outcomes. Rather, it is to affirm the critical value of reimagining student learning outcomes to soberly align our training model with the set of skills that students will need to succeed in the actual classical music marketplace. Again, if we are to prepare aspiring classical music performers for successful careers in the actual marketplace, then our music performance degree must sport a fundamental reorientation toward what supports success in that marketplace.

While each of the previously listed student learning outcomes could be analyzed in length—though their connection to the gathered insights analyzed in this chapter are likely obvious—it seems appropriate to give special attention to the first one on the list. No student learning outcome illuminates the suggested reorientation of the performance degree more powerfully. To confirm, the wording of that first student-learning outcome is requiring the demonstration of a "technically skilled and personal musical voice" certainly affirms the importance of technical mastery in music making. Technique is vital, as we know, because its absence necessarily undermines the very ability of a musician to communicate what she might wish to express. So, importantly, this student-learning outcome affirms that technical skillfulness *is on equal ground with the presence of a strong self-authoring voice.* In this model of training, young musicians are being judged not only according to their technique but also according to their ability and willingness to be courageous and skillful in bringing their interpretive and personal self to the task of performance. Not surprisingly, this first student learning outcome directly aligns with insights from higher education and music/arts industry leaders gathered in this volume, insights that further affirm the desperate need in the field for musicians who aren't (to put it crudely) reproducers of content but rather musicians with a highly personal voice and vision, musicians who come with openness and authenticity to the task of engaging with their audiences and the changing marketplace.

We face a deeper and still more humanistic reason for including and focusing on the "personal musical voice" attribute, and it has to do with the one thing that seems most glaringly (and offensively) missing from our current model of training: respect for the student's personhood. Our students have a right to expect that we will respect their personal voice, and they have a right to expect that their financial investment in a professionally oriented performance degree will truly prepare them for the priorities and landscape of the actual current marketplace. We have, it would seem, a moral obligation to meet both those expectations.

To be clear, the performance degree suggested by the suggested student learning outcomes is *not* aimed at preparing a student for a career landscape that has long passed—a landscape that rewarded artists who had a very specific skill set and orientation toward a standardized sound and music making of a type appropriate to land them a full-time position within a large ensemble, or to succeed at a major competition, or to gain employment as music teacher in a typical university or secondary school in large measure to further reproduce the dominant and traditional training regime. Perhaps no one has described that traditional training model better than the musicologist S. McClary did a few decades ago, when she wrote the following:

> The performers on whom we rely to flesh out notated scores into sound are trained not to interpret (understood as the imposition of the unwanted self on what is fantasized to be a direct transmission of the composer's subjective intentions to the listener), but rather to strive for a perfect, standard sound, for an unbroken, polished surface. Such performers became ideal in the nineteenth century as grist for the symphony orchestra in which the conductor usurped complete control over interpretation and needed only the assurance of dependable sound production from the laboring musician. In our century of Repetition, they have remained ideal for purposes of the recording industry, which demands perfection and the kind of consistency that facilitates splicing.[38]

This first student learning outcome is perhaps most notable because it supports a model of training where the dual abilities of skillful and personal musical voice, when combined with skillfulness in verbal communication, are *in the service of connecting with and engaging general public audiences*. The relationship of all these skills and areas of competency and knowledge are depicted in Figure 2.1.

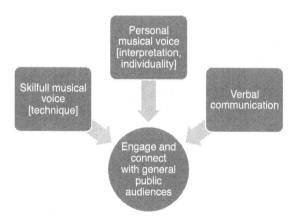

Image 2.1 Proposed Orientation of Music Performance Related Competencies

The issue of connecting with and engaging general public listeners is, as mentioned in the first chapter, a large and complex one. Faculty skeptical of any attempt to evaluate such connection and engagement might well consider that we have access to relevant and helpful models from other arts disciplines. Dance programs such as the one at Shenandoah Conservatory, for example, require dance students to put together an evaluative panel for their performance assessment that includes not only dance faculty but also persons from the community *not* familiar with dance. And students in visual arts degrees are not infrequently expected to gather data from nonprofessional audience surveys as part of larger portfolios required for degree fulfillment. In other words, the work of crafting an appropriate evaluative process to measure "connecting with and engaging general public listeners" will certainly not be easy but is hardly impossible.

An additional note is warranted here regarding the implications that come from a greatly reimagined set of student learning outcomes for a performance degree. Some readers might be excited to consider the ripple effect of a reimagined performance degree would have across all curricula. There is typically a great sharing of core courses and experiences—whether lessons or juries or ensembles or music history/ theory courses—between performance degrees and other music degrees. Given that, there is a good chance that the considerable changes to core courses within a music performance degree would necessarily result in a drastic change to the flavor and focus of the music training within other degrees (e.g., music education, music therapy, music recording). Some faculty, however, might not be so excited by these implications. Their concerns may certainly be warranted. For example, a reimagined performance degree curriculum that aims for the types of student learning outcomes as outlined here might require a variety of *ensemble* experiences that could differ from the type of ensemble experiences that music educators may find themselves still obliged to provide, given state mandates and public school practices. And the type of significant changes to student learning outcomes in a BM performance degree as outlined here might result in a still greater disparity from the type of performance skill training needs of students in, say, a BM Music Therapy program. All of this is to say that a truly honest investigation of the issues being discussed here will give rise to much additional complexity. That potential new complexity does not undermine the importance of pursuing this work. Deep honesty, as the reader knows, often requires great courage, and to be honest in the way we address one issue area might require us to be additionally honest in fixing related issue areas.

Potential Alignment With Core Skills Needed for General Twenty-first-Century Careers

As explained earlier, the shared list of possible student learning outcomes for a performance degree reveals one way that our music training might be reimagined and reoriented to better align with the actual changing music landscape. The list of student learning outcomes provided in this chapter has an additional and final significance worthy of mention here: it appears to be aligned with and supportive of the very skills and personal qualities that business leaders increasingly assert are vital for success in general twenty-first-century careers.

Some readers might be aware of Project Oxygen, the large investigative project Google began in 1998, which aimed to examine factors that might account for the success of its best employees. Its findings were revelatory for many; of the eight most important qualities of Google's top employees, STEM expertise came dead last, and the most important qualities and characteristics were all soft skills, including the ability to communicate and listen well and to convey empathy toward colleagues.[39]

Repeatedly, business leaders have affirmed that the most critical skills for job seekers in twenty-first-century businesses across industry areas are the very type of soft skills and qualities that are privileged in the student learning outcomes list presented here, skills and qualities such as an orientation toward connecting with others, an ability to communicate and engage, curiosity, and creativity.[40]

The implications of all this are exciting. In reorienting the training offered within a music degree to better align with the actual realities of the classical music marketplace, we may not only be offering our students much better preparation for actual career pathways in music but may also be setting them up for greater success within careers across multiple areas in contemporary society.

Notes

1. One thinks, of course, of such volumes as those by Joseph Polisi (Juilliard) and Robert Freeman (Eastman, NEC, and others). See J. W. Polisi, *The Artist as Citizen* (Pompton Plains, NJ: Amadeus Press, 2005); R. Freeman, *The Crisis of Classical Music in America: Lessons from a Life in the Education of Musicians* (Lanham, MD: Rowman & Littlefield, 2014).
2. To confirm, this study built on an understanding of surveying as outlined in O'Leary (2014), sought to employ appropriately worded and distributed questionnaires as advised in Cohen et al. (2011), and employed

focused interviews that were focused as defined within Bell & Waters (2014) and standardized open-ended as defined by McNamara (1999). When interviewees provided author Michael Stepniak with responses to the questions in the context of a Zoom audio interview, the author sought to the follow dominant practice of conducting interviews as outlined in Creswell (2012) and McNamara (no date), for example using probes to gain additional information and undertaking the interview at a time and setting which was comfortable to both parties. See J. Bell and S. Waters, *Doing Your Research Project: A Guide for First-Time Researchers*, 6th ed. (Maidenhead, Berkshire: Open University Press, 2014); L. Cohen, L. Manion, and K. Morrison, *Research Methods in Education*, 7th ed. (New York: Routledge, 2011); J. W. Creswell, *Research Design: Qualitative, Quantitative, and Mixed Methods Approaches*, 3rd ed. (Los Angeles: Sage Publications, 2009); C. McNamara, *General Guidelines for Conducting Interviews*, Free Management Library, 2014, https://managementhelp.org/businessresearch/interviews.htm; Z. O'Leary, *The Essential Guide to Doing Your Research Project*, 2nd ed. (London: Sage Publications, 2013).

3. Angela Myles Beeching, interview with Michael Stepniak, September 28, 2018, transcript.
4. Abra Bush, email message to Michael Stepniak, October 8, 2018.
5. Judy Bundra, email message to Michael Stepniak, November 4, 2018.
6. Fred Bronstein, interview with Michael Stepniak, October 3, 2018, transcript.
7. Robert Cutietta, interview with Michael Stepniak, October 8, 2018, transcript.
8. David Cutler, interview with Michael Stepniak, October 1, 2018, transcript.
9. James Doser, interview with Michael Stepniak, September 28, 2018, transcript.
10. Robert Freeman, interview with Michael Stepniak, October 3, 2018, transcript.
11. Richard Goodstein, email message to Michael Stepniak, September 30, 2018.
12. Tayloe Harding, interview with Michael Stepniak, October 8, 2018, transcript.
13. Paul Hogle, interview with Michael Stepniak, October 8, 2018, transcript.
14. David Myers, interview with Michael Stepniak, October 4, 2018, transcript.
15. Brian Pertl, email message to Michael Stepniak, October 2, 2018.
16. Mary Ellen Poole, email message to Michael Stepniak, October 7, 2018.
17. Greg Sandow, interview with Michael Stepniak, September 27, 2018, transcript.
18. Keith Ward, email message to Michael Stepniak, October 20, 2018.
19. Jenny Bilfield, email message to Michael Stepniak, October 12, 2018.
20. William J. Capone, email message to Peter Sirotin, September 21, 2018.
21. Kristy Edmunds, email message to Peter Sirotin, September 21, 2018.
22. Andrew Lane, email message to Peter Sirotin, October 16, 2018.
23. Stuart Malina, email message to Peter Sirotin, September 24, 2018.
24. André Raphel, email message to Peter Sirotin, November 20, 2018.
25. Courtney Reilly, email message to Peter Sirotin, October 10, 2018.

26. Steve Wogaman, email message to Peter Sirotin, September 19, 2018.
27. John Zion, email message to Peter Sirotin, October 25, 2018.
28. When mention is made of symphony orchestras, most readers might immediately think of the most iconic of those organizations, for example, the New York Philharmonic, Boston Symphony, Los Angeles Philharmonic, Dallas Symphony, or Chicago Symphony. But the fact is that iconic orchestras with budgets typically exceeding $20 million represent only around 2 percent of all the (approximately 1,224) orchestras in the United States. Much more common are orchestras such as those directed by the two conductor interviewees in this study. For further information on the orchestral landscape, see www.arts.gov/sites/default/files/Research-Art-Works-League.pdf.
29. Any reader curious to investigate this further should prepare for a peculiar journey. The list of physical characteristics that appear to impact how individuals are treated within general society and in various workplaces is certainly not a short or simple one. A superficial overview is found in A. Harsch, "Does Attractiveness and Appearance Equate to Leadership and Career Success?," *HuffingtonPost*, September 15, 2017, www.huffingtonpost.com/entry/does-attractiveness-and-appearance-equate-to-leadership_us_59ba734be4b02c642e4a1414. Any examination of this general issue quickly reveals ambiguity and complexity. For example, in certain work environments, greater attractiveness has a very different impact on an individual's perceived assumed competency depending on their gender. See, for example, M. E. Heilman and M. H. Stopeck, "Attractiveness and Corporate Success: Different Causal Attributions for Males and Females," *Journal of Applied Psychology* 70, no. 2 (1985): 379–388.
30. Interestingly, this increasing orientation of audiences toward new experiences aligns with research related to decreasing brand loyalty. For an introduction to the cultural shifts that have resulted in the rapid demise of previously reliable brand loyalty among consumers and the general public, see K. Kusek, "The Death of Brand Loyalty: Cultural Shifts Mean It's Gone Forever," *Forbes*, July 25, 2016, www.forbes.com/sites/kathleenkusek/2016/07/25/the-death-of-brand-loyalty-cultural-shifts-mean-its-gone-forever/#577856e14dde, accessed January 21, 2019. See also L. Tesseras, "The Big Brand Loyalty Theory Is History," *Marketing Week*, January 9, 2013, www.marketingweek.com/2013/01/09/the-big-brand-loyalty-theory-is-history/, accessed January 21, 2019.
31. For an overview of trends and core statistics that affirm the continued growth in giving to such causes as diversity, justice, environment, and human services and public-society benefit organizations, see *The Philanthropy Outlook 2018 & 2019*, February 2018, http://martsandlundy.com/wp-content/uploads/2018/03/Philanthropy_Outlook_2018_2019_RS.pdf. (The Philanthropy Outlook, for example, points to the growing momentum of impact investment, what the report describes as "a growing movement in which investments are made in companies, organizations, and funds for the purpose of creating social or environmental impact in addition to a financial return" (p. 36). See also *11 Trends in Philanthropy for 2019*, Dorothy A. Johnson Center for Philanthropy,

January 15, 2019, www.gvsu.edu/gvnow/2019/johnson-center-experts-predict-11-trends-for-philanthropy-10863.htm; D. Callahan, *Philanthropy Forecast 2018: Trends and Issues to Watch: Inside Philanthropy.* www.insidephilanthropy.com/home/2018/1/7/philanthropy-forecast; and *Online Giving Statistics: The Ultimate List of Charitable Giving Statistics for 2018*, https://nonprofitssource.com/online-giving-statistics/.

32. Although responses from higher education and music/arts industry leaders have been combined in this analysis, responses from the two groups of participants did not show any significant difference in levels of agreement. That is to say, there was considerable variety in the responses within each of the two groups, just as there was in the responses of all participants when the responses of the two groups were combined.

33. See R. Nason, *It's Not Complicated: The Art and Science of Complexity in Business* (Toronto: University of Toronto Press, 2017). Also see R. Nason, "It's Not Complicated," *RMA Journal* 93, no. 6 (March 2011): 66–69.

34. To confirm, the analysis and argument in this section are pursued with an eye to what appear to be dominant and shared understandings of curriculum (as both formal and informal learning experiences that are especially structured and planned by faculty) and student learning outcomes (as the dominant focal points of degrees, and points of assessment as dictated by regional assessment associations/bodies). For all that, the authors do acknowledge that there continues to be great debate among curriculum researchers regarding the exact definition of the very word "curriculum." Perhaps no one has put the vivacity of the debate around the definition of curriculum into greater light than J. T. Dillon when he wrote the following: "Taken as an ensemble the definitions and conceptions of curriculum are known to be incoherent, and by individual contrast to be divergent when not contradictory. It has become obligatory, as in textbooks, to display a dozen or more answers in all their diversity, to almost no purpose or effect other than to dispirit the reader" (p. 344). See J. T. Dillon, "The Questions of Curriculum," *Journal of Curriculum Studies* 41 (June 2009): 343–359.

35. P. T. Ewell, *Accreditation and Student Learning Outcomes: A Proposed Point of Departure*, Council for Higher Education Accreditation, 2001, 6, https://files.eric.ed.gov/fulltext/ED469482.pdf, accessed February 11, 2019. The first mention of Student Learning Outcomes may have been by E. W. Eisner, who proposed SLOs as a goal and assessment point in 1979. See E. W. Eisner, *The Educational Imagination* (New York: Macmillan, 1979), 103. To confirm, the definition that Ewell provided and that has become standard in academic degree programs across the country aligns closely with the curriculum framework proposed by Barnett and Coate, who advocated in 2005 that higher education curriculum should be thought of holistically and should thus encompass three different types of learning: Knowing (knowledge about); Acting (performative knowledge); and Becoming (how knowledge is integrated with the self). See R. Barnett and K. Coate, *Engaging the Curriculum in Higher Education* (Maidenhead: Open University Press and McGraw Hill Education, 2005). On a side note that may be of interest to higher education

music faculty, NASM makes no reference to student learning outcomes in the current handbook. Rather, it references "student learning" eight times, primarily in the following context: "student learning in terms of artistic and academic achievement." See National Association of Schools of Music Handbook 2018–2019, https://nasm.arts-accredit.org/wp-content/uploads/sites/2/2019/01/M-2018-19-Handbook-1-7-2019.pdf. One additional word of acknowledgment is due here: there is ongoing and reasonable argument regarding the appropriateness of student learning outcomes that are behavioral as opposed to nonbehavioral or composite. For an example of the argument against behavioral learning outcomes see J. Allan's writings, including her contention that "the requisite of precise observable objectives in rational curriculum design precludes the planning of earning experiences for which the outcome cannot be pre-stated at a level of specificity capable of being translated into clear-cut behaviours which are capable of being measured and assigned with an indication of what constitutes an acceptable standard of performance in a given context. The reductionist thinking which results from such a prescriptive approach imposes a strait-jacket on curriculum planning; this is the major source of criticism of behavioural objectives" (p. 96). J. Allan, "Learning Outcomes in Higher Education," *Studies in Higher Education* 21, no. 1 (1996): 93–108.

36. "Boston University Academics," *Family and Medical Leave Act (FMLA) | Human Resources*, www.bu.edu/academics/cfa/programs/performance/bm/, accessed February 16, 2019.
37. "Music," Wartburg College, http://catalog.wartburg.edu/preview_entity.php?catoid=7&ent_oid=190&returnto=389, accessed February 16, 2019.
38. See p. 152 of S. McClary, "Afterward: The Politics of Silence and Sound," in *Noise: The Political Economy of Music*, edited by J. Attali (Minneapolis: University of Minnesota Press, 1985), 149–160.
39. V. Strauss, "The Surprising Thing Google Learned About Its Employees: And What It Means for Today's Students," *Washington Post*, December 20, 2017, https://q8rkuwu1ti4vaqw33x41zocd-wpengine.netdna-ssl.com/conservatory/files/2018/09/The-surprising-thing-Google-learned-about-today's-students.pdf, accessed February 12, 2019. For further info on the updated effort at Google, see https://rework.withgoogle.com/blog/the-evolution-of-project-oxygen/.
40. See, for example, C. Beaton, "Top Employers Say Millennials Need These 4 Skills in 2017," *Forbes*, January 6, 2017, https://q8rkuwu1ti4vaqw33x41zocd-wpengine.netdna-ssl.com/conservatory/files/2018/09/Top-Employers-Say-Millennials-Need-These-4-Skills-in-2017.pdf, accessed February 12, 2019; G. Beach, "Hard-Pressed by Soft Skills, CIOs Face Talent Challenge," *CIO Journal, Wall Street Journal*, June 26, 2018, https://q8rkuwu1ti4vaqw33x41zocd-wpengine.netdna-ssl.com/conservatory/files/2018/09/Hard-Pressed-by-Soft-Skills-CIOs-Face-Talent-Challenge.pdf, accessed February 12, 2019; L. Entis, "This Is the No. 1 Thing These CEOs Look For in Job Candidates," *Fortune*, March 26, 2017, https://q8rkuwu1ti4vaqw33x41zocd-wpengine.netdna-ssl.com/conservatory/files/2018/09/This-is-the-No.-1-Thing-CEOs-Look-For-in-Job-Candidates.pdf, accessed February 12, 2019; C. Gallo, "A Global

AI Expert Identifies the Skills You Need to Thrive in the Next 15 Years," *Forbes*, October 4, 2018, https://q8rkuwu1ti4vaqw33x41zocd-wpengine. netdna-ssl.com/conservatory/files/2018/10/A-Global-AI-Expert-Identifies-the-Skills-You-Need-to-Thrive-in-the-Next-15-Years.pdf, accessed February 12, 2019.

Bibliography

"11 trends in philanthropy for 2019." *Grand Valley State University*, January 15, 2019. Accessed February 12, 2019. www.gvsu.edu/gvnow/2019/johnson-center-experts-predict-11-trends-for-philanthropy10863.htm.

Allan, J. "Learning Outcomes in Higher Education." *Studies in Higher Education* 21, no. 1 (1996): 93–108. doi: 10.1080/03075079612331381487.

Barnett, R. and K. Coate. *Engaging the Curriculum in Higher Education*. Maidenhead, England: Open University Press and McGraw Hill Education, 2005.

Beach, G. "Hard-Pressed by Soft Skills, CIOs Face Talent Challenge." *Wall Street Journal*, June 26, 2018. Accessed February 12, 2019. https://q8rkuwu1 ti4vaqw33x41zocd-wpengine.netdna-ssl.com/conservatory/files/2018/09/Hard-Pressed-by-Soft-Skills-CIOs-Face-Talent-Challenge.pdf.

Beaton, C. "Top Employers Say Millennials Need These 4 Skills in 2017." *Forbes*, January 6, 2017. Accessed February 12, 2019. https://q8rkuwu1 ti4vaqw33x41zocd-wpengine.netdna-ssl.com/conservatory/files/2018/09/Top-Employers-Say-Millennials-Need-These-4-Skills-in-2017.pdf.

Bell, J. and S. Waters. *Doing Your Research Project: A Guide for First-Time Researchers* (6th ed.). Maidenhead, Berkshire: Open University Press, 2014.

Bivin, D., U. Osili, A. Pruitt, J. Bergdoll, T. Skidmore, S. Zarins, X. Kou. *The Philanthropy Outlook 2018 & 2019*. Report. Marts & Lundy and Lilly Family School of Philanthropy, Indiana University. Indianapolis, IN: IU LFSP, 2018. http://martsandlundy.com/wpcontent/uploads/2018/03/Philanthropy_Outlook_2018_2019_RS.pdf.

Callahan, D. "Philanthropy Forecast 2018: Trends and Issues to Watch." *Inside Philanthropy*, January 7, 2018. www.insidephilanthropy.com/home/2018/1/7/philanthropy-forecast.

Cohen, L., L. Manion, and K. Morrison. *Research Methods in Education* (7th ed.). New York: Routledge, 2011.

Creswell, J.W. *Research Design: Qualitative, Quantitative, and Mixed Methods Approaches* (3rd ed.). Los Angeles, CA: Sage, 2009.

Dillon, J.T. "The Questions of Curriculum." *Journal of Curriculum Studies* 41, no. 3 (2009): 343–359.

Eisner, E.W. *The Educational Imagination*. New York, NY: Macmillan, 1979.

Entis, L. "This Is the No. 1 Thing These CEOs Look for in Job Candidates." *Fortune*, March 26, 2017. Accessed February 12, 2019. https://q8rkuwu1ti 4vaqw33x41zocd-wpengine.netdna-ssl.com/conservatory/files/2018/09/This-is-the-No.-1-Thing-CEOs-Look-For-in-Job-Candidates.pdf.

Ewell, P.T. *Accreditation and Student Learning Outcomes: A Proposed Point of Departure.* Report. U.S. Department of Education, Council for Higher Education Accreditation. Accessed April 6, 2019. https://files.eric.ed.gov/fulltext/ED469482.pdf.

Freeman, R. *The Crisis of Classical Music in America: Lessons from a Life in the Education of Musicians.* Lanham, MD: Rowman & Littlefield, 2014.

Gallo, C. "A Global AI Expert Identifies the Skills You Need to Thrive in the Next 15 Years." *Forbes*, October 4, 2018. Accessed February 12, 2019. https://q8rkuwu1ti4vaqw33x41zocdwpengine.netdnassl.com/conservatory/files/2018/10/A-Global-AI-Expert-Identifies-the-Skills-You-Need-to-Thrive-in-the-Next-15-Years.pdf.

Harrell, M. and L. Barbato. "Great Managers Still Matter: The Evolution of Google's Project Oxygen." *ReWork*, February 27, 2018. Accessed April 6, 2019. https://rework.withgoogle.com/blog/the-evolution-of-project-oxygen/.

Harsh, A. "Does Attractiveness and Appearance Equate to Leadership and Career Success?" *Huffington Post*, September 15, 2017. www.huffingtonpost.com/entry/does-attractiveness-and-appearance-equate-to-leadership_us_59ba734be4b02c642e4a1414.

Heilman, M.E. and M.H. Stopeck. "Attractiveness and Corporate Success: Different Causal Attributions for Males and Females." *Journal of Applied Psychology* 70, no. 2 (1985): 379–388. doi: 10.1037/0021-9010.70.2.379.

Kusek, K. "The Death of Brand Loyalty: Cultural Shifts Mean It's Gone Forever." *Forbes*, July 25, 2016. Accessed January 21, 2019. www.forbes.com/sites/kathleenkusek/2016/07/25/the-death-of-brand-loyalty-cultural-shifts-mean-its-gone-forever/#577856e14dde.

McClary, S. "Afterward: The Politics of Silence and Sound." In *Noise: The Political Economy of Music*, ed. J. Attali, 149–60. Minneapolis, MN: University of Minnesota Press, 1985.

McNamara, C. "General Guidelines for Conducting Interviews." *Free Management Library.* 2014. https://managementhelp.org/businessresearch/interviews.htm.

Nason, R. "It's Not Complicated." *RMA Journal* 93, no. 6 (2011): 66–69.

Nason, R. *It's Not Complicated: The Art and Science of Complexity in Business.* Toronto, Canada: University of Toronto Press, 2017.

"National Association of Schools of Music Handbook 2018–2019." *National Association of Schools of Music.* Accessed January 7, 2019. https://nasm.arts-accredit.org/wp-content/uploads/sites/2/2019/01/M-2018-19-Handbook-1-7-2019.pdf.

O'Leary, Z. *The Essential Guide to Doing Your Research Project* (2nd ed.). London: Sage, 2013.

Polisi, J.W. *The Artist as Citizen.* Pompton Plains, NJ: Amadeus Press, 2005.

Strauss, V. "The Surprising Thing Google Learned about Its Employees: And What It Means for Today's Students." *The Washington Post*, December 20, 2017. Accessed February 12, 2019. https://q8rkuwu1ti4vaqw33x41zocdwpengine.netdna-ssl.com/conservatory/files/2018/09/The-surprising-thing-Google-learned-about-today%E2%80%99s-students.pdf.

Tesseras, L. "The Big Brand Loyalty Theory is History." *Marketing Week*, January 9, 2013. Accessed January 21, 2019. www.marketingweek. com/2013/01/09/the-big-brand-loyalty-theory-is-history/.

"The Ultimate List of Charitable Giving Statistics for 2018." *NonProfit-Source*. Accessed April 6, 2019. https://nonprofitssource.com/online-giving-statistics/.

Voss, Z.G., G.B. Voss, K. Yair, and K. Lega. *Orchestra Facts: 2006–2014*. Report. National Center for Arts Research, Southern Methodist University. Dallas, TX: SMU NCAR, 2016. Accessed April 8, 2019. www.arts.gov/sites/default/files/Research-Art-Works-League.pdf.

3 Why This Change Is Unusually Difficult
Three Specific Factors May Be Thwarting the Will and Ability of Music Leaders to Change Performance Training Models

Why is it that we so rarely hear of music schools or programs that have made significant change to their performance degree curriculum and are now better preparing graduating students for the current marketplace?[1] And why is it that any collective efforts to spur understanding or advancement in this area nationwide—whether sponsored by such organizations as College Music Society (CMS) or National Association of Schools of Music (NASM)—have seemingly yielded little collective and innovative action around curriculum change among higher education music faculty and leaders nationwide?[2] There are certainly many factors that can create difficulty for higher education music leaders seeking to navigate and enable large-scale change, including the type of programmatic, curricular, and pedagogic changes that the previous chapters suggest are greatly needed. As the examination that follows reveals, however, music leaders in higher education may face three factors that are especially effective in undermining action and progress. Each of those factors is likely well known to music school deans and program administrators. When combined (as they necessarily are for the leaders referenced here), there is a good chance that they can cause a veritable paralysis in action.

I. Daily Distraction by an Unprecedented Scope of Challenges and Level of Change Facing Nonprofit Higher Education Communities and Their Leaders/Administrators

For many years, researchers and education leaders have been describing and lamenting the range and scope of challenges swamping nonprofit higher education institutions and their leaders and administrators. (For a broader selection of literature which includes reference to various aspects of the changing landscape facing higher education both within the United States and internationally, see Appendix A.) The growing scope of those pressures and challenges have led many to be skeptical of the future of the higher education sector. In December 2017, for example, Moody's Investors Service revised its outlook for the higher education sector from stable to negative.[3] Reflecting on the increasingly perilous landscape facing higher education and following the completion of an analysis of 20 years of freshman-enrollment data at more than 1,000 schools, the *Wall Street Journal* noted in 2018 that "colleges and universities are segregating into winners and losers—with winners growing and expanding and losers seeing the first signs of a death spiral." And *Education Dive*, noting the acceleration of closures, mergers, and acquisitions of higher education institutions since 2016, has recently begun keeping an updated and comprehensive list of colleges and universities that have closed.[4]

Most readers of this monograph are likely familiar with the landscape described here. A mere half-dozen of the most dominant of the pressures and challenges present within that work landscape are listed in Table 3.1 and then further described.

Few challenges are currently mentioned as frequently on campuses around the country as those associated with recruitment and enrollment, the financial lifeblood of virtually all higher education institutions. After many years of growth in the number of high school graduates and growth in the enrollment of traditional college-age students, the population of undergraduate students (potential and enrolling) is declining and shows no sign that it will return to its high point. In 2013, the population of 18–24-year-olds was at a historic high of 31.6 million; by 2016 it had dropped to 30.5 million.[5] That number continues to decline,[6] and that slow decline in undergraduate

Table 3.1 The Tidal Wave of Challenges Facing Leaders in Nonprofit Higher Education

1. Critical and growing threats to enrollment numbers
2. Diminishing financial resources
3. Crisis of college affordability and student debt load
4. Mounting expenses related to property, plant, equipment, government legislation and reporting, and student services
5. Ongoing and increasing disruptions to faculty pedagogy and teaching practice
6. Practical and existential challenges from rapid technological change

enrollment (reflecting the ongoing stagnation in high school graduates) is projected to continue until at least 2030–31.[7] By the 2016–2017 academic year, it appeared that more than 60 percent of all higher education institutions were failing to meet their enrollment goals.[8] The problem of declining numbers of U.S.-born students within higher education is further compounded by the fact that the overall number of international graduate applications and first-time enrollment in non-profit higher education institutions have also begun declining, with arts and humanities areas being hurt more than either business and engineering.[9]

Even while challenges are mounting related to enrollment, institutions are facing diminishing financial resources. After a high in 2006–2007, total revenues per full-time-equivalent (FTE) student (specifically from federal and state levels) has continued to fall, especially for four-year degree-granting institutions. Indeed, for just the three years between 2009 and 2012, state appropriations alone declined by more than 14 percent.[10] As the senior director of research and policy analysis at National Association of College and University Business Officers (NACUBO) put it recently, "net-tuition revenue, which accounts for the bulk of funding for private institutions, has been flat or declining for the last five years."[11]

Meanwhile, rising tuition costs and ever-growing student loan debt burdens have not only taken center stage in public and media criticism of higher education but show no signs of slowing. Yes, an increasing number of institutions pursue desperate and symbolic measures (including tuition resets) that might signal fiscal prudence and responsibility, but those actions seem radically out of sync with the scope of this growing challenge. The following statistics are among the many that illuminate the scope of this challenge. Between 1985 and 2013, tuition costs in the United States increased 538 percent as compared with a 121 percent increase in consumer prices.[12] In its 2014 *Higher Education Survey* report, KPMG noted that more than 70 percent of private higher education leaders and more than 60 percent of public higher education leaders cited lack of college affordability as a leading factor negatively and further impacting enrollment.[13] Especially worrisome is the growing realization that the debt and default rate is disproportionally hurting minority students. A Brookings Institution study published in 2018 showed that the debt and default rate among black college students had reached "crisis levels" and that black BA graduates defaulted at more than five times the rate of white BA graduates (21 percent versus 4 percent).[14]

Even while facing enrollment challenges, diminishing financial resources, and pressures to reduce tuition costs and student loan burdens, nonprofit higher education institutions have faced mounting expenses related to property, physical plant and equipment, and an ever-expanding suite of student services. In both public and private institutions, costs of deferred maintenance have seemingly reached critical levels. In 2012 alone, the Chronicle of Higher Education cited estimates by experts that **deferred maintenance** on **college campuses** amounted "to about $36-billion across the country."[15] Institutions have also faced increasing costs related to reporting and data management, including as mandated by government regulation. Frustrated with higher education costs and a seeming lack of accountability for such wrongs as low graduation rates and the turnout of too many seemingly unprepared-for-the-workplace workers, government agencies have increasingly turned to legislation and regulation to prod higher education institutions into greater accountability. Recent acts have included the 2017 Borrower Defense to Repayment Rule,[16] the 2017 College Transparency Act,[17] and the 2014 Gainful Employment Rule[18] (enacted during the Obama presidency and then rescinded under President Trump). With a combination of increasing expenses around all of these areas, it is not surprising that institutions have been forced to devote an ever-decreasing portion of expenditure to teaching faculty. As one noted economist reflected recently, "a typical university around 1970 would have allocated 40% directly for instruction, mostly professor salaries . . . nowadays, it's more like 30%."[19]

There is an additional challenge. Institutions continue to hire researchers and artists familiar primarily with *traditional* pedagogy practice. Yet the dominant model of instruction and pedagogy is undergoing multiple disruptions, including a push for competency-based learning, work-based learning, condensed degrees, prior learning credit, Massive Open Online Courses (MOOCs), personalized learning, condensed degrees, outsourcing of education services, new or revamped delivery modalities and distance learning, and partnership between industry and institutions (often negotiated by senior administrators rather than faculty) resulting in new forms of credentials.[20]

If all of this weren't enough, higher education institutions are also at the center of the practical and existential challenges stemming from the extraordinary changes in technology. While technology has further vitalized some aspects of higher education (most notably academic research),[21] the fact is that the cost of institutional investment in and maintenance of technology and the pace of technological change are greatly disrupting virtually every aspect of life and work. Indeed, the growing impact of automation, digitalization, and advances in artificial intelligence has practical implications on an institution's bottom financial line. (What new software platform that is heralded to faculty as a final solution to a problem doesn't signal a cascade of new required maintenance costs and upcoming purchases?) That growing technological change also places great pressure on higher education institutions to anticipate how to train a global workforce that might be increasingly displaced by those technological advances. Though beyond the scope of this study, it might be worth affirming the scale of that impending disruption. A McKinsey Global Institute report from early 2018, for example, estimated that by 2030 as many as 375 million workers—more than 14 percent of the global workforce—may need to switch occupational categories because of ongoing disruption caused by AI, automation, and related technologies.[22] Although some may feel relief that our challenge within higher education is "simply" to identify what areas won't be threatened by automation or AI, the fact is that this changing technological landscape will likely be perniciously disruptive for some time to come. Y. Harari is among those who seems prudent in warning that "the AI revolution won't be a single watershed event after which the job market will just settle into a new equilibrium. Rather it will be a cascade of ever-bigger disruptions."[23] He goes on to outline a still more frightening scenario:

> Even if we could constantly invent new jobs and retrain the workforce, we may wonder whether the average human will have the emotional stamina necessary for a life of such endless upheaval. . . . As the volatility of the job market and of individual careers increases, would people be able to cope? . . . By 2050 a "useless" class might emerge not merely because of an absolute lack of jobs or lack of relevant education, but also becomes of insufficient mental stamina.[24]

Harari's sobering forecast is hardly singular in the field. The futurist Martin Ford has similarly pointed out that while people were previously able to adapt to periods of large and disruptive technological change, the current technological revolution is occurring at a pace greater than what most people need in order to learn critical new skills.[25]

To be clear, this list of a half-dozen major challenges facing nonprofit higher education institutions and their leaders is only a partial list. It would be difficult enough for the typical music school dean or similar senior leader to have a firm grasp of *the scope and particulars* of such challenges and pressures. But senior academic leaders are now being routinely hired with the expectation that they will not only understand the full scope and particulars of those challenges (a heroic achievement in itself) but also possess the ability and skills to lead change in response to those challenges. The expectation that those academic leaders might cleverly work with others to create plans for change is further made problematic by an additional obstacle. Put simply, even while leaders within nonprofit higher education institutions face myriad challenges and pressures such as those as noted here, those institutions retain a culture that greatly inhibits the ability of their members and leaders to successfully pursue significant and rapid programmatic or organizational change. That culture, quite familiar to the readers of this monograph, is briefly described next.

II. A Unique Combination of Factors That Makes Nonprofit Higher Education Institutions Uniquely Averse to Rapid or Large-Scale Organizational or Programmatic Change

The factors previously outlined are enough to cause the music school dean or music executive distraction and occasional moments of panic. But things are trickier still; that same leader faces a work landscape and organizational culture unusually unsupportive of and resistant to efforts to effect rapid and significant change. As many scholars and higher education critics have helped illuminate over the years, nonprofit higher education institutions possess a unique combination of attributes that make them awkwardly equipped to support the pursuit and adoption of any significant and fast-paced internal change.[26]

While there is no clear agreement on what combination of factors make nonprofit higher education institutions so resistant to change, the combination described below (and summarized in Table 3.2) seems especially effective in blocking any leader's or faculty group's initiative for nimble and innovative action around large-scale change, as would be needed for the type of curricular and pedagogical repositioning that is suggested in this monograph.

As noted, one of the ways that nonprofit higher education institutions stand out among organizations is their possession of an extraordinary number of stakeholders (e.g., students, alumni, parents of current students, board of trustees, presidents, administrative leaders, faculty, staff, local businesses and national businesses, local community, local schools, academic and research bodies, government officials). And the relationship of those different stakeholders to power and to legitimacy in affecting decision making is often unclear, including among the very same stakeholders.[27] The complexity that arises

Table 3.2 Higher Education: A Perfect Combination of Attributes to Block
Large and Quick Programmatic or Organizational Change

---

1. There exist an extraordinary number of stakeholders, with varying
   and unclear relationship to power and legitimacy in affecting decision
   making.
2. Not only are authority and decision making distributed (and complicated
   by a shared governance system), but there are multiple and competing
   power and authority structures.
3. The decision-making process surrounding the evaluation, approval, and
   implementation of proposed significant changes to degree programs and
   curriculum—the organizing units that both frame the central work of
   teaching/learning and reflect core disciplinary and institutional values—is
   typically lengthy and complicated.
4. Orientation to any radical change is further retarded by such factors
   as the following: competition between institutions resulting in faculty
   and administrators having little incentive and inclination to cooperate
   with other institutions; a values-driven culture that supports normative
   arguments often trumping data-driven analysis; and the presence of
   reward structures and budget allocation systems that typically reward the
   status quo over risk-taking or radical innovation.

---

from this reality is further realized when one notes that almost no two
of those stakeholder groups would answer such questions as "Who
is the customer?" or "What is the product" in like manner. (Indeed,
some stakeholders would be as likely to bristle at the relevance of these
questions as others would be to assume that the answers were clear.)

Not only are authority and decision making distributed (and often
unclearly so), but the decision-making process is slowed and made
more complex by each institution's idiosyncratic and often morphing
version of a shared governance system. That system may be democratic
in aspiration, but it is hardly equitable. While faculty in that system
may have power as affirmed by tenure and influence in ultimate decision making, they typically have very little administrative authority
and few resources to support investigative and planning action. A
provost, for example, may have multiple administrative assistants to
support effective management of projects and communication, while
an entire faculty senate body will typically have no dedicated administrative staff support.[28] And, beyond this, higher education institutions
sport multiple and typically competing power and authority structures
(from boards and presidents to faculty and the faculty senate, school
deans and directors, the business/administrative unit versus academic
units, deans, and so on), often pursuing very different outcomes and
goals.[29]

Building on this point, the decision-making processes surrounding the evaluation, approval, and implementation of proposed large changes to curriculum (such as new program proposals or significant alterations to current degree programs) are typically lengthy and complicated. It is not uncommon for the process of new-program approval to take two to three years and to require 10-plus steps (with some public institutions also further requiring review and approval by a politically appointed state board). Beyond involving processes that are lengthy and complicated, curriculum change processes also seem geared less toward innovation than they are to rewarding alignment with standard disciplinary practice.[30]

Nonprofit higher education institutions are unsupportive of radical change for at least three additional reasons.[31] First, institutions exist in a culture of increasingly fierce competition with other similar institutions for students and faculty, making cooperation between faculty and institutions awkward if not downright impossible and further diminishing institutions' capacity to tackle large-scale challenges to a field in a uniform manner. Second, institutional environments and cultures remain values-driven, with faculty often more committed to their department or discipline than to their institution and value judgments and normative arguments playing as important a role in decisions regarding change as hard data.[32] And third, reward and budget allocation systems (for both individual faculty and departments and units) tend to reinforce the status quo rather than promote innovation or change. For faculty, for example, the rewards (whether funding for scholarship-related travel or promotion and tenure) are typically more oriented to supporting activities linked to traditional demonstrations of disciplinary expertise than to encouraging and underwriting initiatives related to disruption and innovation.

III. The Unique Culture Surrounding Classical Music in the Academy; One That Makes that Disciplinary Area Especially Averse to Major Change

As though it weren't enough for leaders in higher education to face an extraordinary range of challenges and be within organizations and cultures that are resistant to the pursuit of large and swift change, the music school dean or program director who seeks to enable and support large-scale programmatic change faces an additional (and too often unacknowledged) obstacle. Specifically, if she is situated within a school that is focused especially on classical music, as most conservatories and schools of music and music departments continue to be, she will likely find herself situated within a community and culture that may be particularly averse to change.

Consider that in most fields and areas within higher education, empirical evidence and critique routinely shape and reshape dominant attitudes and paradigms. Most faculty members in hard sciences and humanities are comfortable with the idea that Sir Isaac Newton's or Immanuel Kant's contributions to human knowledge and understanding can be venerated and at the same time critically challenged and considered outdated in many aspects. Most film and theater faculty will have a similar attitude toward masterpieces and leading historical figures in their respective traditions. As far as the authors of this volume can tell, however, our classical music community (including that found within the typical higher education music school or program) appears to have difficulty in simultaneously honoring and reshaping its relationship to dominant figures, traditions, and paradigms. It might be argued that no performing arts field has as intense and reverential an orientation toward historical and iconic works and figures in its past as we have within classical music. We are, it seems, more likely to hold assumptions that have gone unchallenged for an unusually extended period of time and are likely to honor veneration over personal inquiry and tradition over innovation. This orientation is illuminated in many ways, including such as examples as follows.

Few areas of expertise are more honored in the classical music field since the early 1800s (and the dawn of performers from Paganini to Liszt) than that of performance.[33] Yet even while many classical music lovers continue to idolize virtuosic performers, there is repeated and extensive evidence that the very qualities seemingly prized are often hardly the objective qualities imagined. As findings from such studies as those discussed later reveal, we share a greater tendency to venerate expertness and icons within classical music than is warranted by our ability to undertake an evaluation of them.

In the past two decades, quite a few studies have shown that value judgments even among internationally recognized experts in classical music are highly suspect and far from objective; indeed, research has repeatedly shown that those judgments are subject to a number of factors such as immediacy bias in settings such as competitions[34] and subconscious favoring of visual cues over auditory information.[35] For example, studies have repeatedly shown that listeners tend to rate the musical quality of performers higher if those same performers are judged to be more physically attractive. This shouldn't be surprising since numerous studies have affirmed that visual information typically supersedes auditory information. For example, Tsay's fine study demonstrated that people could more reliably select the actual winners of live music competitions if they relied on silent video recordings of competitors, and the vast majority of both musical novices and professional musicians were unable to identify the winners on the basis of sound recording or recordings with both video and sound.[36] Despite such groundbreaking revelations as these, the number of international classical music competitions continues to grow.[37]

Also illuminating the conservative orientation of our field is the fact that we continue to largely ignore (or sometimes wear as a badge of honor) the extraordinary disparity that has grown and exists between the reverence typically shown within our music programs for historical iconic works and figures from the classical music tradition and the regard that is shown for same by the general public. Van der Merwe captured that disparity well when he reflected that "for the general public, 'classical music' belongs mainly to the eighteenth and nineteenth centuries, carries on with rapidly diminishing vigor into the first few decades of the twentieth, and has ceased to exist by 1950."[38] The cultural and demographic shifts that have moved classical music from a culturally dominant, privileged position to a place of competition with both popular commercial genres and independent, folk, world music, can be perceived as existential threat by a community built on the idea of "timeless" body of musical masterpieces. Lydia Goehr captured the values of that community well when she explained that "classical music is not only regarded as quintessentially civilized, but as the only kind of music that is."[39] The urge among some to keep iconic classical music works and figures in their perceived rightful place (against that assigned by the general public) continues to give rise to a veritable industry of writing and publishing.[40] The public's response, as noted in the opening chapter of this book, has in good measure been to simply give their money and attention elsewhere. And a growing number of observers point out that most general-public listeners view classical music as either irrelevant or an exotic oddity. (See, for example the article in a recent *American Scholar* volume titled "The Sound of Evil: How Did Classical Music in Movies and Television Become Synonymous with Villainy?")[41]

The inherent conservativeness around classical music has also often been affirmed by programming at the annual conferences and gatherings promoted by dominant organizations (NASM, CMS, Chamber Music America, or the like). A review of any typical conference schedule will usually reveal at least one presentation or discussion devoted to audience development that is, in the end, concerned with the peculiarly sentimental and paternalistic question of how we might better entice audiences to appreciate and benefit from the inherent and special beauty found within our repertoire. (The focus in those discussions, it seems, is always on figuring out how to continue doing what we do but to better manipulate others so that they are more likely to appreciate and pay for what we have to offer.) In his keynote speech at the 2014 Chamber Music America National conference, Eric Booth reflected on that very mindset, sharing that someone had once told him that "if orchestras played just two percent better our new audience problem would be solved." He went on to describe and decry the idea that "there really is a belief in some—and it's a kind of traditional mindset—that the perfection of the offering is the answer to this problem."[42] It's impossible here not to ask: What makes us so beholden to tradition and so venerating of the past that we continually ask how to get others to like the masterworks performed in the appropriate manner that we believe is appropriate for them to appreciate and honor?[43]

The conservative orientation of the classical music field writ large is certainly reflected in the dominant and continuing models of apprenticeship training common to classical musicians and captured in the most famous of evaluative moments from that training regimen—the jury moment during which the merit of an aspiring musician is evaluated according to a rubric that largely ignores depth of feeling or honesty of expression and dispassionately evaluates instead such things as the student's technique and grasp of historically informed interpretation. That is to say, it evaluates many factors except for the one thing that has made all music (including classical music of bygone eras) recognizably music—sounds uttered *from the heart*.[44]

An additional and unique aspect of training evident in most music departments and schools is the multiyear apprenticeship and relationship that a student has with a major instrument teacher. A teacher is often touted as belonging to a particular tradition or stemming from a certain pedagogical lineage. The deep emotional bond around these relationships and its impact on aesthetic values lasts for years and sometimes one's entire career. That legacy of tradition casts a long shadow and certainly makes individuals less accepting of change which might threaten or depart from core features of those traditions.

Although there isn't room here to review it in detail, it should be noted that one of the most investigated issues during the past few decades relating to the conservative quality of the culture surrounding classical music has centered not around pedagogy and canon but around questions of gender and race.[45] Certainly one of the many reasons we should not be surprised that the iconic figures in classical music composition, conducting, and higher education leadership remain so disproportionally white and male is the gendered and racial understandings of heroic and individual creativity and intellectualism. Pointing to the gender and race biases that are still to be found in the culture being discussed here, McAndrew and Everett explained that male classical music composers "have an advantage because they look like people's preconceptions of what a composer looks like."[46] And Yang reflected a belief held by many classical music devotees (as Asian classical music performers will often report) when she stated the following:

> Asians have the technique, Westerners have the heart, the soul. The image of Asians as automatons, robots without souls, appears frequently in the Western imagination.[47]

The focus of typical classical music degree programs—on great composers and performers of the past and on teaching students to produce historically informed performances of masterpieces—certainly appears rigid and admitting of little change. With priorities inexorably tied to artistry and artists (both with a capital A), there seems little interest and space in typical music programs and schools for any corresponding investigation into any number of potentially ripe matters for inquiry, including the use of recent technological advances to clarify just how much the size, acoustics or the room, instruments used, variation in dynamic range, and shared cultural references account for in a physiologically and psychologically satisfying musical experience.

In a 2007 essay published in *New Republic* in which he considered a number of polemical volumes arguing for a retained and privileged place for classical music in contemporary society, Taruskin advised that there were two ways of dealing with the sort of growing pressures classical musicians faced to, as he put it, go out and earn their living.[48] He described one "accommodation, which can entail painful losses and suffer from its own excesses (the dumbing down that everybody except management deplores)," and he explained that the other way was "to hole up in such sanctuary as still exists and hurl imprecations and exhortations." Those two ways do not represent the only options we have. There is another option, one that truly honors the joy of music making that has always accompanied it at its fullest, the type of joy-full musicianship that is being privileged in this volume. That third option is for us to better enable and support the rising next generation of musicians (including those who love the classical repertoire wholly or in part) to make the music that they have an aching to make and do all in our power to provide them with the best possible set of skills and knowledge appropriate for the music marketplace they will need to navigate.

To be clear, there is no wish here to brook the right that each lover of the classical music cannon has to cherish experiences that might be found in the midst of listening to or performing works from the traditional classical cannon. It is absolutely understandable that performers as well as listeners gathered within a formal concert venue might feel awe and heartbreak within the Cavatina movement of Beethoven's monumental Op.130 string quartet. Or that certain listeners, when hearing a recording (any recording) of Elisabeth Schwazkopf's performance of "September" from Richard Strauss's *Four Last Songs* will feel amazement and even transcendence at her entry and delivery of the magical line "Sommer Lächelt erstaunt und matt." And it is understandable that a not insignificant number of opera lovers have traveled the globe in hopes of catching tenor Jonas Kaufmann at his next scheduled performance.

While these things are understandable, there is something anachronistic (and perhaps even mean-spirited) when a personal revelry in the glories of a genre of music morphs into an unbending orientation of reverence that is pressed upon others. It seems that within the academy, we have (for the most part) collectively moved to such an orientation. The spirit of spontaneity and experimentation, of reveling in the emotional connection between listener and performer that was at the core of now-cherished classical music eras (whether Bach's, Mozart's, or Verdi's) is too absent when our work as educators turns to the question of what we might privilege in the academy. Though they are judgmental to be sure, the observations by McAlpin (writing in the early 1920s) still rings true:

> the musical expert may know all about the technical difficulties ... the theoretic constitution ... that in itself is a possible source of danger. It renders him liable to concentrate on structure and technique, rather than on the underlying meaning of music. Indeed, many a learned professor has so fastened on the science of his art as to deaden his soul to the spontaneous freshness of inspired beauty.[49]

Some readers might decry the tone and message here as an example of attempts to water down the training and undermine the integrity of the educational efforts and orientation of music faculty. To be absolutely clear, the argument here is not one of belittling situations where expert performers and expert listeners engage within a concert space. There are few experiences that the authors of this volume have prized more than when they have had the opportunity to perform and engage with listeners who (for their part) brought a wide base of musical knowledge and reference and were simultaneously open and focused on receiving new musical information. Such exchanges are the stuff of dreams for many classical musicians and occur rarely. In making the argument that is outlined in this volume, we are simply asserting that such rarified experiences—unusual as they might be in contemporary society—are hardly the only experiences worthy of pursuit by students.

Notes

1. Readers are likely familiar with the examples of curricular innovation already mentioned in chapter one. Among them are those found in the University of Southern California's ReDesign initiative, in the DePauw curricular redesign (and the 21st Century Musician initiative), and in Peabody Institute's Breakthrough Curriculum. For details regarding curricular change at USC Thornton, see "The ReDesign," USC Thornton School of Music, https://music.usc.edu/redesign/, accessed February 20, 2019. For details on curricular change at DePauw's School of Music, including around 21st Century Musician concepts, see "School of Music," DePauw University, www.depauw.edu/academics/school-of-music/, accessed February 20, 2019. And for details on curricular change at Peabody, see "Peabody Breakthrough Curriculum," Johns Hopkins University, Peabody Institute, https://peabody.jhu.edu/academics/breakthrough-curriculum/, accessed February 20, 2019.
2. One of the most famous of sponsored reports remains the following: D. Myers, E. Sarath, J. Chattah, L. Higgins, V. Levine, D. Rudge, and T. Rice, *Transforming Music Study from Its Foundations: A Manifesto for Progressive Change in the Undergraduate Preparation of Music Majors Report of the Task Force on the Undergraduate Music Major.* Report. College Music Society, 2014.
3. "US Higher Education Sector Outlook Revised to Negative as Revenue Growth Prospects Soften," *Moody's,* December 5, 2017, www.moodys.com/research/Moodys-US-higher-education-sector-outlook-revised-to-negative-as-PR_376587, accessed February 20, 2019.
4. For the latest update (from January 29, 2019), see H. Busta, "How Many Colleges and Universities Have Closed Since 2016?," *Education Dive,* January 29, 2019, www.educationdive.com/news/how-many-colleges-and-universities-have-closed-since-2016/539379/.
5. See W. J. Hussar and T. M. Bailey, *Projections of Education Statistics to 2024,* Table B-4, U.S. Department of Education, 2016.
6. P. Fain, "Enrollment Slide Continues, at Slower Rate," *Inside Higher Ed,* December 20, 2017, www.insidehighered.com/news/2017/12/20/national-enrollments-decline-sixth-straight-year-slower-rate, accessed February 19, 2019.
7. Western Interstate Commission for Higher Education, *Knocking at the College Door: Projections of High School Graduates,* Report, 2016, https://knocking.squarespace.com/reports/2017/3/22/full-report.

8. S. Jaschik, and D. Lederman, "2016 Survey of College and University Admissions Directors," *Inside Higher Ed*, 2016, www.insidehighered. com/booklet/2016-survey-college-university-admissions-directors.

9. Council of Graduate Schools, "For the First Time in over a Decade, International Graduate Applications and Enrollments Decline at U.S. Institutions," *News Release*, January 30, 2018. CGSnet, https://cgsnet. org/ckfinder/userfiles/files/Intl_Survey_Report2017_release_final.pdf, accessed February 19, 2019. Included in that document was the following acknowledgment of the possible relationship between federal administration actions and those enrollment trends: "Recent changes in immigration policy, including the executive order barring entry or return of U.S. visa holders from specific countries, are being closely watched by members of the graduate education community. While students directly affected by the ban constitute a relatively small percentage of international graduate students, there has been significant concern that new immigration policies will tarnish the U.S.'s image as a welcoming destination for international students and scholars."

10. National Center for Education Statistics (NCES), "Digest of Education Statistics, 2014," 2016. https://nces.ed.gov/programs/digest/2014menu_tables.asp, accessed February 19, 2019.

11. M. Valbrun, "Tuition Conundrum," *Inside Higher Ed*, April 30, 2018, www.insidehighered.com/news/2018/04/30/nacubo-report-finds-tuition-discounting-again, accessed February 19, 2018.

12. M. Jamrisko and I. Kolet, "College Costs Surge 500% in U.S. since 1985: Chart of the Day," *Bloomberg Business*, August 26, 2013, www.bloomberg.com/news/articles/2013-08-26/college-costs-surge-500-in-u-s-since-1985-chart-of-the-day, accessed February 19, 2019.

13. M. McGuirt and D. Gagnon, "2014 Higher Education Outlook Survey: A Syllabus for Transformation," *KPMG Higher Ed Industry*, 2014, https://institutes.kpmg.us/content/dam/institutes/en/government/pdfs/2014/2014-higher-ed.pdf.

14. J. Scott-Clayton, *The Looming Student Loan Default Crisis Is Worse Than We Thought*, Economic Studies, The Brookings Institute, Vol. 2, no. 34 (Washington, DC: Brookings Institute, 2018), www.brookings.edu/wp-content/uploads/2018/01/scott-clayton-report.pdf.

15. S. Carlson, "How the Campus Crumbles: Colleges Face Challenges from Deferred Maintenance," *Chronicle of Higher Education*, May 20, 2012, www.chronicle.com/article/How-the-Campus-Crumbles/131920 accessed February 19, 2019.

16. "Borrower Defense to Repayment," *Federal Student Aid*, April 29, 2018, https://studentaid.ed.gov/sa/repay-loans/forgiveness-cancellation/borrower-defense, accessed February 19, 2019.

17. O. G. Hatch, "S.1121-115th Congress (2017–2018): College Transparency Act," *Congress.gov*, May 15, 2017, www.congress.gov/bill/115th-congress/senate-bill/1121, accessed February 19, 2019..

18. A. Kreighbaum, "For-Profits Keep Access to Billions in Aid," *Inside Higher Ed*, August 13, 2018, www.insidehighered.com/news/2018/08/13/dropping-gainful-employment-means-profits-keep-billions-student-aid, accessed February 19, 2019.

19. Economist Richard Vedder, as quoted in H. Hoffower, "College Is More Expensive Than It's Ever Been, and the 5 Reasons Why Suggest It's Only Going to Get Worse," *Business Insider*, July 8, 2018, www.businessinsider. com/why-is-college-so-expensive-2018-4 accessed February 19, 2019.

20. This is but a partial list of the typical array of challenges facing faculty wishing to teach and further refine their pedagogy practice. For a further list, see M. S. Andrade, "A Responsive Higher Education Curriculum: Change and Disruptive Innovation," *Innovations in Higher Education: Cases on Transforming and Advancing Practice*, November 5, 2018, doi: 10.5772/intechopen.80443, accessed February 19, 2019. A note about online learning: at the same time that current faculty and colleges struggle to attract traditional students, there is growing competition among institutions to attract full- and part-time students through online offerings. Indeed, the number of students taking at least one distance education class grew by more than 17 percent between 2012 and 2016. See "New Study: Over Six Million Students Now Enrolled in Distance Education," *OLC*, May 2, 2017, https://onlinelearningconsortium.org/news_item/new-study-six-million-students-now-enrolled-distance-education/, accessed February 19, 2019.

21. See, for example, W. W. Ding, S. G. Levin, P. E. Stephan, and A. E. Winkler, "The Impact of Information Technology on Scientists Productivity, Quality, and Collaboration Patterns," *Management Science* 56, no. 9 (2010): 1439–1461, doi: 10.3386/w15285, accessed February 19, 2019; J. J. Duderstadt, "Change and the Research University," *EDUCAUSE Review* (May 9, 2012), http://er.educause.edu/articles/2012/5/change-and-the-research-university, accessed February 19, 2019; S. Vincent-Lancrin, "What Is Changing in Academic Research? Trends and Futures Scenarios," *European Journal of Education* 41, no. 2 (May 12, 2006): 169–202, doi: 10.1111/j.1465-3435.2006.00255.x, accessed February 19, 2019.

22. P. Illanes, S. Lund, M. Mourshed, S. Rutherford, and M. Tyreman, "Retraining and Reskilling Workers in the Age of Automation," McKinsey Global Institute, January 2018, www.mckinsey.com/~/media/McKinsey/Featured%20Insights/Future%20of%20Organizations/Retraining%20and%20reskilling%20workers%20in%20the%20age%20of%20automation/Retraining-and-reskilling-workers-in-the-age-of-automation.ashx, accessed February 19, 2019.

23. Y. N. Harari, *21 Lessons for the 21st Century* (London: Penguin Random House, 2018), 32.

24. Harari, *21 Lessons for the 21st Century*, 32.

25. M. Ford, "The Rise of the Robots: Impact on Unemployment and Inequality," in *Confronting Dystopia: The New Technological Revolution and the Future of Work*, edited by E. Paus (Ithaca: Cornell University Press, 2018), 27–45. There are, of course, economists who downplay the potential disruption of the current technological on employment. See, for example, Oren Cass's ode to the worker and to a rosy vision of future employment in *The Once and Future Worker: A Vision for the Renewal of Work in America* (New York: Encounter Books, 2018).

26. Example of works offering better insights into aspects of that complicated landscape include the following: P. G. Altbach, R. O. Berdahl, and P. J. Gumport, *Higher Education in American Society*, 3rd ed. (Amherst,

NY: Prometheus Books, 1994); M. N. Bastedo, P. G. Altbach, and P. J. Gumport, *American Higher Education in the Twenty-First Century: Social, Political, and Economic Challenges*, 4th ed. (Baltimore, MD: Johns Hopkins University Press, 2016); J. L. Buller, *Change Leadership in Higher Education: A Practical Guide to Academic Transformation* (San Francisco, CA: Jossey-Bass, 2015); C. M. Christensen, J. P. Burkholder, and H. J. Eyring, *Innovative University: Changing the DNA of Higher Education from the Inside Out* (San Francisco, CA: Jossey-Bass, 2011); P. Cohen, "The Crisis of the University," *Campus Review* (2004): 9–12; M. D'Ambrosio and R. G. Ehrenberg, *Transformational Change in Higher Education: Positioning Colleges and Universities for Future Success* (Cheltenham, UK: Edward Elgar, 2007); R. M. Diamond, "Why Colleges Are So Hard to Change," *Inside Higher Ed*, September 8, 2006, www. insidehighered.com/views/2006/09/08/why-colleges-are-so-hard-change, accessed February 19, 2019; H. A. Giroux, "Academic Entrepreneurs: The Corporate Takeover of Higher Education," *Tikkun* 20, no. 2 (2005): 18–20, www.questia.com/magazine/1P3-805243291/academic-entrepre neurs-the-corporate-takeover-of, accessed February 19, 2019; A. J. Kezar, *How Colleges Change: Understanding, Leading, and Enacting Change* (New York: Routledge, 2014); W. Krull, "Who Is Leading Whom, Where to, What for, and How? Governance and Empowerment in the University of the Twenty-First Century," in *Universities in Change: Innovation, Technology, and Knowledge Management*, edited by A. Altmann and B. Ebersberger (New York: Springer, 2012), 117–133; J. Lumby, "Leadership and Power in Higher Education," *Studies in Higher Education* (April 2, 2018): 1–11, doi: 10.1080/03075079.2018.1458221, accessed February 19, 2019; A. McKay, "The Future of Higher Education in the United States," unpublished whitepaper, Shenandoah University, August 1, 2018; F. Newman, L. Couturier, and J. Scurry, *The Future of Higher Education: Rhetoric, Reality, and the Risks of the Market* (San Francisco, CA: Jossey-Bass, 2004); L. Randall, "Transforming a University: A Study of Process Leadership," *Academy of Educational Leadership Journal* 16, no. 2 (2012): 1–20, www.abacademies.org/articles/aeljvol16no22012. pdf, accessed February 19, 2019; S. Rizvi, K. Donnelly, and M. Barber, "An Avalanche Is Coming: Higher Education and the Revolution Ahead," *Institute for Public Policy Research*, June 12, 2017, www.ippr.org/ publications/an-avalanche-is-coming-higher-education-and-the-revolution-ahead, accessed March 1, 2018; F. Rochford, "Is There Any Clear Idea of a University?," *Journal of Higher Education Policy and Management* 28, no. 2 (January 22, 2007): 147–158, doi: 10.1080/13600800600750988, accessed February 19, 2019; D. J. Rowley, H. D. Lujan, and M. G. Dolence, *Strategic Change in Colleges and Universities: Planning to Survive and Prosper* (San Francisco, CA: Jossey-Bass, 2001); E. P. St. John, and M. D. Parsons, eds., *Public Funding of Higher Education: Changing Contexts and New Rationales* (Baltimore, MD: Johns Hopkins University Press, 2004); R. Zemsky, *Checklist for Change: Making American Higher Education a Sustainable Enterprise* (New Brunswick, NJ: Rutgers University Press, 2013).

27. For a broader discussion of stakeholders, see especially C. Chapleo and C. Simms, "Stakeholder Analysis in Higher Education," *Perspectives: Policy*

and *Practice in Higher Education* 14, no. 1 (January 26, 2010): 12–20, doi: 10.1080/13603100903458034, accessed February 20, 2019; also O. Avci, E. Ring, and L. Mitchelli, "Stakeholders in U.S. Higher Education: An Analysis Through Two Theories of Stakeholders," *Journal of Knowledge Economy and Knowledge Management* 10, no. 2 (2015): 45–54, http://dergipark.gov.tr/download/article-file/323147, accessed February 20, 2019.

28. Many presidents and board members at private and public higher education institutions appear to be struggling with understanding how to value shared governance (which honors faculty involvement in much decision making) while being increasingly tempted to simply centralize most decision making around the most senior administrators and thereby become more responsive to change and the changing marketplace. (Faculty at some institutions might depict the quality of engagement by executives around shared governance not as struggling with but scheming around.) Trying to find a middle ground between shared governance and executive leadership, a recent report from the American Council on Education and the Center for Public Research and Policy explained that "a volatile financial environment, the rise of international partnerships, greater accountability pressures, the need for new business models, new technologies, and changing demographics are just some of these challenges, which call for leadership solutions that are tested both inside and outside of higher education." They went on to explain that "shared leadership is different from shared governance. Shared governance is based on the principles of faculty and administration having distinct areas of delegated authority and decision making. Shared leadership, by contrast, is more flexible and identifies various individuals on campus with relevant expertise. This allows multiple perspectives rather than those of a single decision-making body; for example, only faculty or administration." See A. J. Kezar and E. M. Holcombe, *Shared Leadership in Higher Education: Important Lessons from Research and Practice* (Washington, DC: American Council on Education, 2017). For additional investigation and analysis on this topic, see Association of Governing Boards of Universities and Colleges, "Shared Governance: Changing With the Times," whitepaper, March, 2017. See also S. S. Cowen, "Shared Governance Does Not Mean Shared Decision Making," *Chronicle of Higher Education*, August 13, 2018, www.chronicle.com/article/Shared-Governance-Does-Not/244257, accessed February 20, 2019.

29. It is not uncommon to hear faculty (from both large and small, public and private universities) reveal the disconnect between what their university's latest strategic plan is purportedly pursuing and the work that their own school or unit is focusing on.

30. As far as the authors can tell, there is no sweeping study that illuminates all the barriers that are faced by individuals and units that would pursue bold curricular change. One better examination of the multiple barriers that seem to exist around pursuing and implementing curricular change can be found in Trudi Cooper's 2017 article, though her study is set within the Australian higher education environment. The barriers she identifies include not only large ones—the tensions between new curriculum frameworks and the tacit curriculum embedded in university

processes and practices, the presence of insufficient time to fully implement the scope of change needed—but also the myriad associated challenges: changes to affected pedagogy, interaction with institutional systems and practices, problems with documenting new curriculum within institutional systems, educating students about new approaches to learning and how they differed from previous experiences and expectations, and faculty development to ensure shared understanding of the intention of the new curriculum and ensure adjustment to the ways they taught. See T. Cooper, "Curriculum Renewal: Barriers to Successful Curriculum Change and Suggestions for Improvement," *Journal of Education and Training Studies* 5, no. 11 (November 25, 2017): 115–128, doi: 10.11114/jets.v5i11.2737, accessed February 20, 2019. For a report of an institution that reshaped its curriculum review process to enable more nimble consideration and approval, see M. S. Andrade, "A Responsive Higher Education Curriculum: Change and Disruptive Innovation," *Innovations in Higher Education: Cases on Transforming and Advancing Practice*, November 5, 2018, doi: 10.5772/intechopen.80443, accessed February 20, 2019. A number of curriculum change–related studies are also helpfully described in the unusually exhaustive annotated bibliography compiled by the University of Michigan in the early 2000s. See M. W.Peterson, M. K. McLendon, A. D. Anderson, S. Tarbox, and L. Park, *Change and Transformation in Higher Education*, Center for the Study of Higher and Postsecondary Education, University of Michiga, 2nd ed. (Ann Arbor: University of Michigan, 2001), https://pdfs.semanticscholar.org/8aa1/8ca93307bb1915e2c97b88d0f10449463b72.pdf accessed February 20, 2019.

31. The observations in this section draw especially on A. J. Kezar, *Understanding and Facilitating Organizational Change in the 21st Century: Recent Research and Conceptualizations* (San Francisco, CA: Jossey-Bass, 2001), and from R. M. Diamond, "Why Colleges Are So Hard to Change," *Inside Higher Ed*, September 8, 2006, www.insidehighered.com/views/2006/09/08/why-colleges-are-so-hard-chang, accessed February 19, 2019.

32. Most higher education institutions, it might be fair to posit, possess a disconnected and fraught dual identity as mission-driven organizations (grounded in shared values and aspirations) and business (with customers and processes and seemingly hard bottom lines). And expert full-time and tenured faculty often retain many aspects of what might be called a freelancer or subcontractor status in other organizational settings—a leading expert who pursues work sometimes for the employing institution but often beyond it. Note, for example, the extraordinary range of faculty policies on conflict of commitment and interest that exists at all larger institutions.

33. Among the many notable work that situate the rise of the virtuoso artist as newly dominant within society are P. Metzner, *Crescendo of the Virtuoso: Spectacle, Skill, and Self-Promotion in Paris during the Age of Revolution* (Berkeley: University of California Press, 1998); S. Bernstein, *Virtuosity of the Nineteenth Century: Performing Music and Language in Heine, Liszt, and Baudelaire* (Stanford, CA: Stanford University Press, 1998); Z. Cvejić, *The Virtuoso as Subject: The Reception of Instrumental*

Virtuosity, c. 1815–c. 1850 (Newcastle, England: Cambridge Scholars Publishing, 2016). Though not directly related, the following also provides interesting context to the nineteenth century's increasing fascination with the spectacular performance: D. Cavicchi, *Listening and Longing: Music Lovers in the Age of Barnum* (Middletown, CT: Wesleyan University Press, 2011).

34. V. Ginsburgh, "Awards, Success and Aesthetic Quality in the Arts," *Journal of Economic Perspectives* 17, no. 2 (2003): 99–111, doi: 10. 1257/089533003765888458, accessed February 20, 2019.

35. There are multiple studies affirming the visual bias that listeners have for evaluating the music performers viewed. For a taste, see R. Kopiez and F. Platz, "When the Eye Listens: A Meta-Analysis of How Audio-Visual Presentation Enhances the Appreciation of Music Performance," *Music Perception: An Interdisciplinary Journal* 30, no. 1 (2012): 71–83, doi: 10.1525/mp.2012.30.1.71, accessed February 20, 2019; C. Ryan and E. Costa-Giomi, "Attractiveness Bias in the Evaluation of Young Pianists' Performance," *Journal of Research in Music Education* 52, no. 2 (2004): 141–154, doi: 10.2307/3345436, accessed February 20, 2019; C. Ryan, J. Wapnick, N. Lacaille, and A. Darrow, "The Effects of Various Physical Characteristics of High-Level Performers on Adjudicators' Performance Ratings," *Psychology of Music* 34, no. 4 (2006): 559–572, doi: 10.1177/0305735606068106, accessed February 20, 2019; J. Wapnick, L. Campbell, J. Siddell-Strebel, and A. Darrow, "Effects of Non-Musical Attributes and Excerpt Duration on Ratings of High-Level Piano Performances," *Musicae Scientiae* 13, no. 1 (2009): 35–54, doi: 10.1177/1029864909013001002, accessed February 20, 2019; J. Wapnick, A. Darrow, J. Kovacs, and L. Dalrymple, "Effects of Physical Attractiveness on Evaluation of Vocal Performance," *Journal of Research in Music Education* 45, no. 3 (1997): 470–479, doi: 10.2307/3345540, accessed February 20, 2019; J. Wapnick, J. Kovacs-Mazza, and A. Darrow, "Effects of Performer Attractiveness, Stage Behavior, and Dress on Violin Performance Evaluation," *Journal of Research in Music Education* 46, no. 4 (1998): 510–521, doi: 10.2307/3345347, accessed February 20, 2019; J. Huang and C. L. Krumhansl, "What Does Seeing the Performer Add? It Depends on Musical Style, Amount of Stage Behavior, and Audience Expertise," *Musicae Scientiae* 15, no. 3 (2011): 343–364, doi: 10.1177/1029864911414172, accessed February 20, 2019.

36. See C. J. Tsay, "Sight Over Sound in the Judgment of Music Performance," *Proceedings of the National Academy of the Sciences of the United States of America* 110, no. 36 (September 3, 2013): 14580–14585, doi: 10.1073/pnas.1221454110, accessed February 20, 2019.

37. The reverential (and largely critique-free) stance toward what constitutes great (and stylistically permissible) performance within classical music is certainly seen within what Taruskin in his essay "On Letting Music Speak for Itself" called the "musicological" approach toward performance; a type of stance that (beyond owing much to romantic historicism with its unquestioning deference to the past) is revealed especially in the not-uncommon admonition within classical music communities of "letting the music speak for itself," an idea that Taruskin explains places the score in a strangely illogical position of privilege and "implies hostility, contempt,

82 *Why This Change Is Unusually Difficult*

or at least mistrust of performers." R. Taruskin, "On Letting Music Speak for Itself," in *Text and Act: Essays on Music and Performance* (New York: Oxford University Press, 1995), 51–66.

38. P. van der Merwe, *Roots of the Classical: The Popular Origins of Western Music* (New York: Oxford University Press, 2004), 463.

39. See L. Goehr, *The Imaginary Museum of Musical Works: An Essay in the Philosophy of Music* (New York: Oxford University Press, 2007), 245.

40. One thinks of such volumes as the following: J. Johnson, *Who Needs Classical Music? Cultural Choice and Musical Value* (New York: Oxford University Press, 2002); J. Fineberg, *Why Bother? Hear the World of Contemporary Culture Through a Composer's Ears* (New York: Routledge, 2006); L. Kramer, *Why Classical Music Still Matters* (Berkeley: University of California Press, 2007). And, to an extent, J. Horowitz, *Classical Music in America: A History of Its Rise and Fall* (New York: Norton, 2005), or any number of articles throughout the twentieth century asserting the supremacy of classical music over other musics. A more recent example of those (unintendedly hyperbolic) articles is J. Young, "How Classical Music Is Better than Popular Music," *Philosophy* 91, no. 4 (2016): 1–18.

41. T. Gioia, "The Sound of Evil: How Did Classical Music in Movies and Television Become Synonymous with Villainy?," *American Scholar* 88, no. 2 (Spring 2019): 99–103.

42. See E. Booth, "Conference Keynote Address," *Address, 2014 Chamber Music America National Conference*, New York, 2014. Quote taken from 15:30–15:57 in recording: https://vimeo.com/86634516.

43. With apologies to Robert Louis Stevenson, it seems that the work of meeting listeners from the general public where they are in locations where they are comfortable with programming that they might enjoy as much as we might wish to perform it is an undertaking too simple and too inconsequential for individuals of our heroic mold; we would rather set ourselves up to fight to the last breath the work of civilizing those around us into our image—distinguished by possession of a sophisticated appreciation of our cherished genre of music. Though not well known, the work referenced here is a golden basket of gentle admonitions. R. L. Stevenson, *A Christmas Sermon* (New York: Charles Scribner's Sons, 1900). The actual Stevenson quotes referenced include the following: "We require higher tasks, because we do not recognise the height of those we have. Trying to be kind and honest seems an affair too simple and too inconsequential for gentlemen of our heroic mould; we had rather set ourselves to something bold, arduous, and conclusive; we had rather found a schism or suppress a heresy, cut off a hand or mortify an appetite. But the task before us, which is to co-endure with our existence, is rather one of microscopic fineness, and the heroism required is that of patience. . . . There is an idea abroad among moral people that they should make their neighbours good. One person I have to make good: myself. But my duty to my neighbour is much more nearly expressed by saying that I have to make him happy—if I may."

44. Jacques Barzun was perhaps pointing to that very thing—"heart-ness"— when he observed that "if music merely tickled the ear, it would still be agreeable, but it would remain a trifling pastime." J. Barzun, "Is Music

Unspeakable?," in *A Jacques Barzun Reader* (New York: Harper Collins, 2002), 328.

45. Of course the references here are multiple, with the body of related literature and critique exploding beginning in the late 1980s and early 1990s. One of the most accessible introductions to classical music's relationship to such concepts and constructs as race, gender, and class is found in C. Scharff, *Gender, Subjectivity, and Cultural Work: The Classical Music Profession* (London: Routledge, 2018). Among the more detailed investigations of related issues are those found in the following leading works: I. Biddle and K. Gibson, eds., *Masculinity and Western Musical Practice* (Farnham, England: Ashgate Publishing, 2009); C. E. Blackmer and P. J. Smith, eds., *En Travesti: Women, Gender Subversion, Opera* (New York: Columbia University Press, 1995); J. Bowers and J. Tick, eds., *Women Making Music: The Western Art Tradition, 1150–1950* (Urbana: University of Illinois Press, 1987); M. J. Citron, "Gender, Professionalism, and the Musical Canon," *Journal of Musicology* 8, no. 1 (1990): 102–117, doi: 10.2307/763525, accessed February 20, 2019; S.C. Cook and J. S. Tsou, eds., *Cecilia Reclaimed: Feminist Perspectives on Gender and Music* (Urbana: University of Illinois Press, 1994); S. G. Cusick, "Gender and the Cultural Work of a Classical Music Performance," *Repercussions* 3, no. 1 (1994): 77–110, www.ocf.berkeley.edu/~repercus/wp-content/uploads/2011/07/repercussions-Vol.-3-No.-1-Cusick-Suzanne-G.-Gender-and-the-Cultural-Work-of-a-Classical-Music-Performance.pdf; M. Leonard, *Gender in the Music Industry* (Aldershot, England: Ashgate Publishing, 2007); M. Clayton, T. Herbert, and R. Middleton, eds., *The Cultural Study of Music: A Critical Introduction* (New York: Routledge, 2011); S. McClary, *Feminine Endings: Music, Gender, and Sexuality*, 2nd ed. (Minneapolis: University of Minnesota Press, 2002); R. A. Solie, ed., *Musicology and Difference: Gender and Sexuality in Music Scholarship* (Berkeley: University of California Press, 1993).

46. See S. McAndrew and M. Everett, "Symbolic Versus Commercial Success Among British Female Composers," in *Social Networks and Music Worlds*, edited by N. Crossley, S. McAndrew, and P. Widdop (Abingdon, England: Routledge, 2015), 64.

47. M. Yang, "East Meets West in the Concert Hall: Asians and Classical Music in the Century of Imperialism, Post Colonialism, and Multiculturalism," *Asian Music* 38, no. 1 (December 2007): 1–30, doi: 10.1353/amu.2007.0025, accessed February 20, 2019. See also her wonderful article on Asian hip hop artists, in which Yang explains that those artists must operate "within the constraints imposed upon Asian American artists generally, between the poles of whiteness and blackness, presence and lack, visibility and invisibility, subject and object." M. Yang, "Yellow Skin, White Masks," *American Academy of Arts and Sciences* 142, no. 4 (2013): 27, doi: 10.1162/daed_a_00232, accessed January 14, 2019.

48. R. Taruskin, "The Musical Mystique: Defending Classical Music Against Its Devotees," *New Republic* 237, no. 8 (October 22, 2007): 34–45, doi: 10.1525/california/9780520249776.001.0001, accessed January 14, 2019.

49. See page 422–423 of C. McAlpin, "On Hearing Music," *Musical Quarterly* 8, no. 3 (1922): 422–423, www.jstor.org/stable/738166, accessed January 14, 2019.

Bibliography

Altbach, P.G., R.O. Berdahl, and P.J. Gumport. *Higher education in American Society* (3rd ed.). Amherst, NY: Prometheus Books, 1994.

Andrade, M.S. "A Responsive Higher Education Curriculum: Change and Disruptive Innovation." In *Innovations in Higher Education: Cases on Transforming and Advancing Practice*, IntechOpen. November 5, 2018.

Association of Governing Boards of Universities and Colleges. 2017. "Shared Governance: Changing with the Times." *Whitepaper*. AGB, March.

Avci, O., E. Ring, and L. Mitchelli. "Stakeholders in U.S. Higher Education: An Analysis Through Two Theories of Stakeholders." *The Journal of Knowledge Economy and Knowledge Management* 10, no. 2 (2015): 45–54. Accessed February 20, 2019. http://dergipark.gov.tr/download/article-file/323147.

Barzun, J. "Is Music Unspeakable?" *A Jacques Barzun Reader* (2002): 324–337.

Bastedo, M.N., P.G. Altbach, and P.J. Gumport. *American Higher Education in the Twenty-First Century: Social, Political, and Economic Challenges* (4th ed.). Baltimore, MD: Johns Hopkins University Press, 2016.

Bernstein, S. *Virtuosity of the Nineteenth Century: Performing Music and Language in Heine, Liszt, and Baudelaire.* Stanford, CA: Stanford University Press, 1998.

Biddle, I. and K. Gibson, eds. *Masculinity and Western Musical Practice.* Farnham, England: Ashgate Publishing, 2009.

Blackmer, C.E. and P.J. Smith, eds. *En Travesti: Women, Gender Subversion, Opera.* New York, NY: Columbia University Press, 1995.

Booth, E. "Conference Keynote Address." Address. 2014 Chamber Music America National Conference. New York, NY, 2014. Quote taken from 15:30–15:57 in recording. https://vimeo.com/86634516.

"Borrower Defense to Repayment." *Federal Student Aid*, April 29, 2018. Accessed February 19, 2019. https://studentaid.ed.gov/sa/repay-loans/forgiveness-cancellation/borrower-defense.

Bowers, J. and J. Tick, eds. *Women Making Music: The Western Art Tradition, 1150–1950.* Urbana, IL: University of Illinois Press, 1987.

Bransberger, P. and D. Michelau. *Knocking at the College Door: Projections of High School Graduates.* Report. Western Interstate Commission for Higher Education. December, 2016. Accessed April 6, 2019. https://knocking.squarespace.com/reports/2017/3/22/full-report.

Buller, J.L. *Change Leadership in Higher Education: A Practical Guide to Academic Transformation.* San Francisco, CA: Jossey-Bass, 2015.

Busta, H. "How Many Colleges and Universities Have Closed since 2016?" *Education Dive*, January 29, 2019. www.educationdive.com/news/how-many-colleges-and-universities-have-closed-since-2016/539379/.

Carlson, S. "How the Campus Crumbles: Colleges Face Challenges from Deferred Maintenance." *The Chronicle of Higher Education*, May 20, 2012. Accessed February 19, 2019. www.chronicle.com/article/How-the-Campus-Crumbles/131920.

Cass, O. *The Once and Future Worker: A Vision for the Renewal of Work in America*. New York, NY: Encounter Books, 2018.

Cavicchi, D. *Listening and Longing: Music Lovers in the Age of Barnum*. Middletown, CT: Wesleyan University Press, 2011.

Chapleo, C. and C. Simms. "Stakeholder Analysis in Higher Education." *Perspectives: Policy and Practice in Higher Education* 14, no. 1 (2010): 12–20.

Christensen, C.M., J.P. Burkholder, and H.J. Eyring. *Innovative University: Changing the DNA of Higher Education from the Inside Out*. San Francisco, CA: Jossey-Bass, 2011.

Citron, M.J. "Gender, Professionalism, and the Musical Canon." *The Journal of Musicology* 8, no. 1 (1990): 102–117.

Clayton, M., T. Herbert, and R. Middleton, eds. *The Cultural Study of Music: A Critical Introduction*. New York, NY: Routledge, 2011.

Cohen, P. "The Crisis of the University." *Campus Review*, 2004.

Cook, S.C. and J.S. Tsou, eds. *Cecilia Reclaimed: Feminist Perspectives on Gender and Music*. Urbana, IL: University of Illinois Press, 1994.

Cooper, T. "Curriculum Renewal: Barriers to Successful Curriculum Change and Suggestions for Improvement." *Journal of Education and Training Studies* 5, no. 11 (2017): 115–128.

Council of Graduate Schools. "For the First Time in Over a Decade, International Graduate Applications and Enrollments Decline at U.S. Institutions." *CGSnet*, News release, January 30, 2018. Accessed February 19, 2019. https://cgsnet.org/ckfinder/userfiles/files/Intl_Survey_Report2017_release_final.pdf.

Cowen, S.S. "Shared Governance Does Not Mean Shared Decision Making." *The Chronicle of Higher Education*, August 13, 2018. Accessed February 20, 2019. www.chronicle.com/article/Shared-Governance-Does-Not/244257.

Cusick, S.G. "Gender and the Cultural Work of a Classical Music Performance." *Repercussions* 3, no. 1 (1994): 77 110. Accessed April 6, 2019. www.ocf.berkeley.edu/~repercus/wp-content/uploads/2011/07/repercussions-Vol.-3-No.-1-Cusick-Suzanne-G.-Gender-and-the-Cultural-Work-of-a-Classical-Music-Performance.pdf.

Cvejić, Z. *The Virtuoso as Subject: The Reception of Instrumental Virtuosity, c. 1815—c. 1850*. Newcastle, England: Cambridge Scholars Publishing, 2016.

D'Ambrosio, M. and R.G. Ehrenberg. *Transformational Change in Higher Education: Positioning Colleges and Universities for Future Success*. Cheltenham, UK: Edward Elgar, 2007.

Diamond, R.M. "Why Colleges Are So Hard to Change." *Inside Higher Ed*, September 8, 2006. Accessed February 19, 2019. www.insidehighered.com/views/2006/09/08/why-colleges-are-so-hard-change.

"Digest of Education Statistics, 2014." *National Center for Education Statistics*, 2016. Accessed February 19, 2019. https://nces.ed.gov/programs/digest/2014menu_tables.asp.

Ding, W.W., S.G. Levin, P.E. Stephan, and A.E. Winkler. "The Impact of Information Technology on Scientists Productivity, Quality, and Collaboration Patterns." *Management Science* 56, no. 9 (2010): 1439–1461.

Duderstadt, J.J. "Change and the Research University." *Educause Review*, May 9, 2012. Accessed February 19, 2019. http://er.educause.edu/articles/2012/5/change-and-the-research-university.

Fain, P. "Enrollment Slide Continues, at Slower Rate." *Inside Higher Ed*, December 20, 2017. Accessed February 19, 2019. www.insidehighered.com/news/2017/12/20/national-enrollments-decline-sixth-straight-year-slower-rate.

Fineberg, J. *Why Bother? Hear the World of Contemporary Culture Through a Composer's Ears*. New York, NY: Routledge, 2006.

Ford, M. "The Rise of the Robots: Impact on Unemployment and Inequality." In *Confronting Dystopia: The New Technological Revolution and the Future of Work*, ed. E. Paus. Ithaca, NY: Cornell University Press, 2018.

Ginsburgh, V. "Awards, Success and Aesthetic Quality in the Arts." The Journal of Economic Perspectives 17, no. 2 (2003): 99–111.

Gioia, Theodore. "The Sound of Evil: How Did Classical Music in Movies and Television Become Synonymous with Villainy?" *American Scholar* 88, no. 2 (2019): 99–103.

Giroux, H.A. "Academic Entrepreneurs: The Corporate Takeover of Higher Education." *Tikkun* 20, no. 2 (2005): 18–20. Accessed February 19, 2019. www.questia.com/magazine/1P3-805243291/academic-entrepreneurs-the-corporate-takeover-of.

Goehr, L. *The Imaginary Museum of Musical Works: An Essay in the Philosophy of Music*. New York, NY: Oxford University Press, 2007.

Harari, Y.N. *21 Lessons for the 21st Century*. London, England: Penguin Random House, 2018.

Hatch, O.G. "S.1121–115th Congress (2017–2018): College Transparency Act." *Congress.gov*, May 15, 2017. Accessed February 19, 2019. www.congress.gov/bill/115th-congress/senate-bill/1121.

Hoffower, H. "College Is More Expensive Than It's Ever Been, and the 5 Reasons Why Suggest It's Only Going to Get Worse." *Business Insider*, July 8, 2018. Accessed February 19, 2019. www.businessinsider.com/why-is-college-so-expensive-2018-4.

Horowitz, J. *Classical Music in America: A History of Its Rise and Fall*. New York, NY: Norton, 2005.

Huang, J. and C.L. Krumhansl. "What Does Seeing the Performer Add? It Depends on Musical Style, Amount of Stage Behavior, and Audience Expertise." *Musicae Scientiae* 15, no. 3 (2011): 343–364.

Hussar, W.J. and T.M. Bailey. *Projections of Education Statistics to 2024*. Report. U.S. Department of Education. 2016.

Illanes, P., S. Lund, M. Mourshed, S. Rutherford, and M. Tyreman. "Retraining and Reskilling Workers in the Age of Automation." *McKinsey Global Institute*, January, 2018. Accessed February 19, 2019. www.mckinsey.com/~/media/McKinsey/Featured%20Insights/Future%20of%20Organizations/Retraining%20and%20reskilling%20workers%20in%20the%20age%20of%20automation/Retraining-and-reskilling-workers-in-the-age-of-automation.ashx.

Jamrisko, M. and I. Kolet. "College Costs Surge 500% in U.S. Since 1985: Chart of the Day." *Bloomberg Business*, August 26, 2013. Accessed

February 19, 2019. www.bloomberg.com/news/articles/2013-08-26/college-costs-surge-500-in-u-s-since-1985-chart-of-the-day.

Jaschik, S. and D. Lederman. "2016 Survey of College and University Admissions Directors." *Inside Higher Ed*, 2016. Accessed April 6, 2019. www.insidehighered.com/booklet/2016-survey-college-university-admissions-directors.

Johnson, J. *Who Needs Classical Music? Cultural Choice and Musical Value*. New York, NY: Oxford University Press, 2002.

Kezar, A.J. *How Colleges Change: Understanding, Leading, and Enacting Change*. New York, NY: Routledge, 2014.

Kezar, A.J. *Understanding and Facilitating Organizational Change in the 21st Century: Recent Research and Conceptualizations*. San Francisco, CA: Jossey-Bass, 2001.

Kezar, A.J. and E.M. Holcombe. *Shared Leadership in Higher Education: Important Lessons from Research and Practice*. Washington, DC: American Council on Education, 2017.

Kopiez, R. and F. Platz. "When the Eye Listens: A Meta-Analysis of How Audio-Visual Presentation Enhances the Appreciation of Music Performance." *Music Perception: An Interdisciplinary Journal* 30, no. 1 (2012): 71–83.

Kramer, L. *Why Classical Music Still Matters*. Berkeley, CA: University of California Press, 2007.

Kreighbaum, A. "For-Profits Keep Access to Billions in Aid." *Inside Higher Ed*, August 13, 2018. Accessed February 19, 2019. www.insidehighered.com/news/2018/08/13/dropping-gainful-employment-means-profits-keep-billions-student-aid.

Krull, W. "Who Is Leading Whom, Where To, What For, and How?: Governance and Empowerment in the University of the Twenty-First Century." In *Universities in Change: Innovation, Technology, and Knowledge Management*, ed. A. Altmann and B. Ebersberger. New York, NY: Springer, 2012.

Leonard, M. *Gender in the Music Industry*. Aldershot, England: Ashgate Publishing, 2007.

Lumby, J. "Leadership and Power in Higher Education." *Studies in Higher Education* (2018): 1–11.

McAlpin, C. "On Hearing Music." *The Musical Quarterly* 8, no. 3 (1922): 422–423. Accessed January 14, 2019. www.jstor.org/stable/738166.

McAndrew, S. and M. Everett. "Symbolic Versus Commercial Success Among British Female Composers." In *Social Networks and Music Worlds*, ed. N. Crossley, S. McAndrew, and P. Widdop. Abingdon, England: Routledge, 2015.

McClary, S. *Feminine Endings: Music, Gender, and Sexuality* (2nd ed.). Minneapolis, MN: University of Minnesota Press, 2002.

McGuirt, M. and D. Gagnon. *2014 Higher Education Outlook Survey: A Syllabus for Transformation*. Report. KPMG Higher Ed Industry. 2014. Accessed April 6, 2019. https://institutes.kpmg.us/content/dam/institutes/en/government/pdfs/2014/2014-higher-ed.pdf.

McKay, A. "The Future of Higher Education in the United States." Unpublished whitepaper. Shenandoah University, August 1, 2018.

Metzner, P. *Crescendo of the Virtuoso: Spectacle, Skill, and Self-Promotion in Paris during the Age of Revolution.* Berkeley, CA: University of California Press, 1998.

Myers, D., E. Sarath, J. Chattah, L. Higgins, V. Levine, D. Rudge, and T. Rice. *Transforming Music Study from Its Foundations: A Manifesto for Progressive Change in the Undergraduate Preparation of Music Majors Report of the Task Force on the Undergraduate Music Major.* Report. Task Force of the Undergraduate Music Major, The College Music Society. 2014. Accessed April 6, 2019. www.mtosmt.org/issues/mto.16.22.1/manifesto.pdf.

"The New Classical." *USC Thornton School of Music.* Accessed February 20, 2019. https://music.usc.edu/redesign/.

Newman, F., L. Couturier, and J. Scurry. *The Future of Higher Education: Rhetoric, Reality, and the Risks of the Market.* San Francisco, CA: Jossey-Bass, 2004.

"New Study: Over Six Million Students Now Enrolled in Distance Education." *Online Learning Consortium,* May 2, 2017. Accessed February 19, 2019. https://onlinelearningconsortium.org/news_item/new-study-six-million-students-now-enrolled-distance-education/.

"Peabody Breakthrough Curriculum." *Johns Hopkins University, Peabody Institute.* Accessed February 20, 2019. https://peabody.jhu.edu/academics/breakthrough-curriculum/.

Peterson, M.W., M.K McLendon, A.D. Anderson, S. Tarbox, and L. Park. *Change and Transformation in Higher Education.* Annotated Bibliography. Center for the Study of Higher and Postsecondary Education, University of Michigan. 2nd ed. Ann Arbor, MI: University of Michigan, 2001. Accessed February 20, 2019. https://pdfs.semanticscholar.org/8aa1/8ca93307bb1915e2c97b88d0f10449463b72.pdf.

Randall, L. "Transforming a University: A Study of Process Leadership." *Academy of Educational Leadership Journal* 16, no. 2 (2012): 1–20. Accessed February 19, 2019. www.abacademies.org/articles/aeljvol16no22012.pdf.

Rizvi, S., K. Donnelly, and M. Barber. "An Avalanche Is Coming: Higher Education and the Revolution Ahead." Institute for Public Policy Research. June 12, 2017. Accessed March 1, 2018. www.ippr.org/publications/an-avalanche-is-coming-higher-education-and-the-revolution-ahead.

Rochford, F. "Is There Any Clear Idea of a University?" *Journal of Higher Education Policy and Management* 28, no. 2 (2007): 147–158.

Rowley, D.J., H.D. Lujan, and M.G. Dolence. *Strategic Change in Colleges and Universities: Planning to Survive and Prosper.* San Francisco, CA: Jossey-Bass, 2001.

Ryan, C. and E. Costa-Giomi. "Attractiveness Bias in the Evaluation of Young Pianists' Performance." *Journal of Research in Music Education* 52, no. 2 (2004): 141–154.

Ryan, C., J. Wapnick, N. Lacaille, and A. Darrow. "The Effects of Various Physical Characteristics of High-Level Performers on Adjudicators' Performance Ratings." *Psychology of Music* 34, no. 4 (2006): 559–572.

Scharff, C. *Gender, Subjectivity, and Cultural Work: The Classical Music Profession*. London, England: Routledge, 2018.

"School of Music." *DePauw University*. Accessed February 20, 2019. www.depauw.edu/academics/school-of-music/.

Scott-Clayton, J. *The Looming Student Loan Default Crisis Is Worse Than We Thought*. Report. Economic Studies, The Brookings Institute. 34th ed. Vol. 2. Washington, DC: Brookings Institute, 2018. Accessed April 6, 2019. www.brookings.edu/wp-content/uploads/2018/01/scott-clayton-report.pdf.

Solie, R.A., ed. *Musicology and Difference: Gender and Sexuality in Music Scholarship*. Berkeley, CA: University of California Press, 1993.

Stevenson, R.L. *A Christmas Sermon*. New York, NY: Charles Scribner's Sons, 1900.

St. John, E.P. and M.D. Parsons, eds. *Public Funding of Higher Education: Changing Contexts and New Rationales*. Baltimore, MD: Johns Hopkins University Press, 2004.

Taruskin, R. "On Letting Music Speak for Itself." In *Text and Act: Essays on Music and Performance*, ed. R. Taruskin, 51–66. New York, NY: Oxford University Press, 1995.

Taruskin, R. "The Musical Mystique: Defending Classical Music against Its Devotees." *New Republic* 237, no. 8 (2007): 34–45.

Tsay, C.J. "Sight over Sound in the Judgment of Music Performance." *Proceedings of the National Academy of the Sciences of the United States of America* 110, no. 36 (2013): 14580–14585.

"US Higher Education Sector Outlook Revised to Negative as Revenue Growth Prospects Soften." *Moody's*, December 5, 2017. Accessed February 20, 2019. www.moodys.com/research/Moodys-US-higher-education-sector-outlook-revised-to-negative-as--PR_376587.

Valbrun, M. "Tuition Conundrum." *Inside Higher Ed*, April 30, 2018. Accessed February 19, 2018. www.insidehighered.com/news/2018/04/30/nacubo-report-finds-tuition-discounting-again.

Van der Merwe, P. *Roots of the Classical: The Popular Origins of Western Music*. New York, NY: Oxford University Press, 2004.

Vincent-Lancrin, S. "What Is Changing in Academic Research? Trends and Futures Scenarios." *European Journal of Education* 41, no. 2 (2006): 169–202.

Wapnick, J., A. Darrow, J. Kovacs, and L. Dalrymple. "Effects of Physical Attractiveness on Evaluation of Vocal Performance." *Journal of Research in Music Education* 45, no. 3 (1997): 470–479.

Wapnick, J., J. Kovacs-Mazza, and A. Darrow. "Effects of Performer Attractiveness, Stage Behavior, and Dress on Violin Performance Evaluation." *Journal of Research in Music Education* 46, no. 4 (1998): 510–521.

Wapnick, J., L. Campbell, J. Siddell-Strebel, and A. Darrow. "Effects of Non-Musical Attributes and Excerpt Duration on Ratings of High-Level Piano Performances." *Musicae Scientiae* 13, no. 1 (2009): 35–54.

Yang, M. "East Meets West in the Concert Hall: Asians and Classical Music in the Century of Imperialism, Post Colonialism, and Multiculturalism." *Asian Music* 38, no. 1 (2007): 1–30.

Yang, M. "Yellow Skin, White Masks." *American Academy of Arts and Sciences* 142, no. 4 (2013): 27.

Young, J. How Classical Music Is Better Than Popular Music. *Philosophy* 91, no. 4 (2016): 1–18.

Zemsky, R. *Checklist for Change: Making American Higher Education a Sustainable Enterprise.* New Brunswick, Canada: Rutgers University Press, 2013.

4 Making Change That Counts

The previous chapter outlined three factors that make it very difficult for leaders within music programs and schools to pursue the type of significant and rapid curricular change within music programs that seems to be needed. Those factors include a higher education landscape that is rife with extraordinary challenges, the unique qualities that make higher education institutions typically inhospitable to rapid or significant change, and a disciplinary field and culture (classical music) that are unusually averse to change, oriented as they are to past traditions and veneration of past icons and paradigms.

This chapter turns to present and examine the insights shared by higher education leaders who participated in the study introduced and described in chapter two. (The names and institutional affiliation of those leaders is listed near the opening of the second chapter.) As was clarified in chapter two, the group of 16 higher education music leaders who participated in the previously described interview study was asked a final question. That question, reproduced below, asked interviewees to provide advice regarding how leaders within music programs and schools might best approach pursuing the type of significant and rapid curricular change that seems to be needed.

This chapter introduces the insights that interviewees shared, revealing emergent themes, then moves to an analysis of responses, and a brief examination of how the points of advice correspond to models of change management. Finally, building on an awareness of the skills and knowledge needed for leaders to competently prepare a community for change and help steer it through that change, the chapter outlines four recommendations. Those recommendations describe ways we could radically elevate the readiness of music faculty and leaders nationwide to undertake leadership and participation in needed change.

Responses Regarding How Higher Education Music Leaders Might Best Enable Significant and Swift Curricular Change

As mentioned, the higher education participants in this interview study were asked a final question:

> "For many good reasons, curricular change in higher education has traditionally required slow and incremental work. A fast-changing performing arts marketplace, however, is demanding we make rapid and large scale curricular changes to offered degrees. What one piece of advice would you share with the music department chair or music school dean wondering how to help her faculty pursue a big/bold reimagining of music performance curriculum to better prepare graduates for that marketplace and full-time employment?"

Perhaps not surprisingly given the complexity and challenge of the task described in that question, all higher education music leaders interviewed offered more than one piece of advice. A close investigation of their responses revealed that a few strategies were especially mentioned.

The tactics or strategies that these higher education leaders advised others to consider in pursuing big/bold changes to curriculum are summarized in Table 4.1 and then described in further detail thereafter.

Table 4.1 Most Mentioned Advice Regarding How Leaders Can Help Faculty Pursue a Big/Bold Reimagining of Music Performance Curriculum

Factor/Issue Area Mentioned	*Number of Mentions*
Provide space for innovative people/work/courses	9 mentions
Pay attention to and ensure good process	7 mentions
Remember that data and examples can drive change	3 mentions
Advocate and communicate	3 mentions
Make sure you are in a supportive context	2 mentions

1. *Provide Space for Innovative People/Work/Courses*

The most commonly shared advice from interviewed higher education leaders was for the leader who desired big and quick curricular change to sidestep the inherent obstacles that necessarily accompanied the curricular change process within the academy and instead provide space for innovative people, work, and/or courses. Director Mary Ellen Poole advised that the best short and long-term strategy was to "hire only people who are willing and able to address this [the needed changes to curriculum and approach]." Faculty leader David Cutler advised that leaders "cultivate leaders [for change] from within," and faculty leader David Myers likewise emphasized the importance of creating space "for dialogue and conversation with those faculty who may be interested in participating in incremental change." And arts leader Greg Sandow spoke of the importance of filling the calendar with moments of mentorship from people who were working innovatively; "bring in musicians who have done this," he explained.

Dean Judy Bundra spoke to the importance of providing space for innovative work when she advised that leaders "find external funding for career initiatives; new courses, guest speakers, workshops." Taking the point further, dean Tayloe Harding pointed to the value of creating new and innovative areas that would naturally draw students: "offer options—new progressive tracks—and let the student movement into those 'alternate' tracks speak." As president Paul Hogle explained, "it's really hard to be innovative in the strictures and formality of tenure roles." He went on: "we need an incubator space, not to operate without *any* roles, but with a freedom and independence that doesn't serve any master but the student career needs."

Dean Tayloe Harding summed up the value of pursuing multiple tactics to create space for change. One powerful strategy, he explained, was "not to make quick change but to build a culture around values that lead to organic and natural changes." He continued by sharing how his school has done "a lot of non-curricular things—who we hire, what type of sentences we put in job descriptions, etcetera."[1]

2. *Pay Attention to and Ensure Good Process*

The second most commonly shared advice from interviewed higher education leaders was for leaders to help shape and manage a process around curriculum change. Interviewees described that leadership work in a number of ways. A number spoke of the need to give faculty special space for investigation and conversations. Dean Fred Bronstein advised that the leader should not only "be relentless" but should "then develop process, seed the culture, continually refine, be patient but not too patient." Dean Rob Cutietta explained that the reason that the faculty at his school had ultimately succeeded in envisioning and embracing a new curriculum was that members had the opportunity to go through a longer process, one grounded in shared values; it was a "long process," he explained, "[they were] doing work-shops, taking retreats, getting . . . excited." Importantly, he shared, that process started "with fundamentals, not credits, nuts and bolts." Faculty leader David Cutler advised that the leader should remember that her job is "not to pitch ideas, but to have process where great ideas can flourish." Director Keith Ward, as quoted below, illuminated the cultural values of the academy when he outlined the core responsi-bilities of the leader wishing to help faculty pursue significant change.

> A leader should help a faculty become familiar with the litera-ture on curricular reform and with initiatives in other programs. From there, frank discussions would explore where a faculty falls in these ongoing reforms and ask how these changes happening in our midst should influence an institution's curricular story. . . . Knowledge of reform should help a faculty find its way in the changing landscape and revise curricula in a way that makes sense to an institution's identity. . . . Faculty members need to see that they have a stake in the process. We ignore change at our own peril, but change imposed from above will not succeed, especially in higher education, where faculty enjoy a high degree of auton-omy. Change needs to be inclusive and organic; it needs a sense of ownership.

Along similar lines, dean Brian Pertl spoke of the importance of both ensuring the process was organic and grounded in an institution's values, and the importance of giving forward-thinking faculty space to create small change.

> First, figure out who you are as an institution . . . before deciding what changes will best work for you. . . . Don't focus on changing the entire curricular structure if you want rapid change. . . . If you have forward-thinking faculty, let them drive the change in the courses they are teaching.

3.   *Remember That Data and Examples Can Drive Change, and Advocate and Communicate*

There were two ideas that tied for third most commonly shared advice from interviewees. One was for the leader aspiring to facilitate signifi-cant curricular change to remember the value and utility of hard data. Repeatedly, interviewees reflected that such impersonal information could not be argued with in the same way that a leader's opinions or advice could. As dean Richard Goodstein explained,

> look at the placement of your graduates, their current job prospects and in what careers their alumni are in 10-years after graduation, and you will learn all you need to know about a mandated overhaul of the performance curriculum. I have no doubt the data will speak for itself.

Dean Fred Bronstein raised a similar point he advised leaders to "do a deep survey of alumni to get information and data about preparation, about strengths and weaknesses [of their preparation within your school's program]."

Interviewees also pointed to the importance of leaders' advocating and communicating for change. Senior associate dean Abra Bush explained that it was critical for the leader to "have a clear and strong vision constantly communicated," while faculty leader David Myers spoke of the need for the leader to be an "articulate spokesperson" for the changes that were emerging as critical.

4. Make Sure You Are in a Supportive Context

Two of the interviewees took time to affirm that there are other factors beyond tactics that can have a large impact on a leader's success in the area of facilitating significant curricular change. As dean Robert Freeman explained, the "dean's length of time in and security within position has an impact; big change can happen when trust is present, time is available, and [the] leader has strong job security." Faculty leader David Myers explained that it also greatly helps to have the right support from above within an institution; "you have to have supportive upper administrators."

5. Other

There were several isolated pieces of advice that interviewees shared. Interestingly, two of those spoke to the difficulty of the work being imagined within the academic culture. Faculty leader David Cutler shared that the work of pursuing big curricular change was "hard unless you create a culture of change." And faculty leader David Myers spoke of the difficulty of having visionary leadership since leadership in the academy "comes traditionally from within" and because the leadership that comes from within typically "can't afford politically to challenge." He went on to explain: "We see a lot of status-quo managers."

Discussion

Like other higher education leaders, leaders overseeing music schools labor in a landscape that is quite antagonistic to the pace and scope of curricular and programmatic changes that seem urgently needed, and in relative isolation.

It should not be surprising that there is an element of heroic improvisation to the substantial change initiatives around curriculum that some of these interviewees described in greater detail—like those described by deans Rob Cutietta, Brian Pertl, and Tayloe Harding. While not possessing any formal training in change leadership and management, the interviewees appeared to share an orientation toward strategic work and clearly (in describing work they had overseen) pointed to the possession of a combination of hard and soft skills. In reflecting on tactics and approaches, they hinted at the work that senior music leaders do. That work included pursuing change with the best understanding available of tactics, within a landscape that includes highly independent and expert faculty and features disciplinary traditions that are highly prized and well developed and resistant to change, and with an organizational culture and quality (as explained later) that is relatively unusual among all types of organizations in this country in terms of its ambivalence (or even hostility) toward significant or rapid change.

As the preceding chapter sought to illuminate, the scope of challenges facing the music executive in nonprofit higher education institution is as formidable as it is extraordinarily complex. It is striking, then, that for all the caveats about context, there was a general positivity in all responses.[2] None of the interviewees, for example, responded with anything approaching despondency, and all replied with points of advice, suggesting that they believed there *were* ways that music leaders might best pursue significant and swift programmatic change.

As some readers may be aware, there is a growing body of research that has sought to identify the organizational dynamics, interpersonal relationships, systems, and leadership traits that together enable one organization to pursue significant change successfully.[3] It should come as little surprise that the advice the interviewees offered aligns in some measure with better-known models of organizational change and change management. Table 4.2 identifies how the points of advice from interviewees relate to a few of the better-known models.

Any analysis of models focusing on change management or leadership for change quickly illuminates that change within organizations is highly complex and (in many ways) unpredictable. And an increasing

Table 4.2 Examples of Change Management Models, and Advice offered by Interviewees

	Summary	*Alignment with advice offered by interviewees?*
Kurt Lewin[4]	*Three-stage process:* **Unfreeze, Change, Refreeze**	**Unfreeze** A number of interviewees referenced the need to prepare faculty for change; for example, to "seed the culture" (dean FB), to pursue a "long process . . . getting faculty excited" (dean RC), and to gather and present data that would support need for change (dean RG).
John Kotter[5]	*Eight-stage process:* **Establish urgency, Create guiding coalition, Develop a change vision, Communicate the vision, Empower others to act, Garner short-term wins, Don't give up, Incorporate changes into culture**	**Empower others to act (most aligned)** As shown at the outset of this chapter, much advice centered around providing space for people to do innovative work. **Communicate the vision and Don't give up** Some offered advice centered around the critical importance of constantly communicating a vision, and there were a few mentions of the importance of patience and perseverance.
Kübler-Ross[6]	*Five-stage process:* **Denial, Anger, Bargaining, Depression, Acceptance**	**Denial, Anger** While not directly mentioned, some of the advice that was offered by higher education leaders (especially as related to providing faculty with space, data, activities to engage and consider options) certainly seems appropriate to efforts that aim to avoid denial (from faculty of need for changes) or anger (by faculty at facing the potential work of changing).

(Continued)

Table 4.2 (Continued)

	Summary	Alignment with advice offered by interviewees?
Michael Fullan[7]	*Five Components of Leadership (necessary to best mobilize those around to effectively tackle difficult change/challenges):* **Moral purpose, Understanding change, Relationship building, Knowledge building, and Coherence making** *These Five Core Leadership Components, when practiced, strengthen three qualities critical in leadership/leaders:* **Energy, Enthusiasm, and Hope**	**Knowledge building** and **Coherence making** While no interviewees spoke specifically to moral purpose, at least one spoke to the importance of understanding change, and several spoke to the importance of providing faculty with the opportunity to build knowledge and understanding and to create space for faculty to struggle with issues and build a more coherent understanding of ways forward. While there were no specific mentions of the personal qualities of energy, enthusiasm, or hope, a number of interviewees (including dean FB, dean AB, dean RC, director KW, and faculty leader GS) spoke of the importance of being highly and persistently engaged around actions supporting change (suggesting a high level of energy and enthusiasm), and all interviewees responded to the question positively, suggesting that they believed it would be reasonable for other music leaders to engage in change leadership with expectations and hope for success.

number of authors have suggested that dominant change management models, while being significantly applicable in hierarchical organizations (such as corporations or the military), might have limited application in higher education, where authority and decision making are distributed. Buller goes so far as to assert that "the very concept of change management is a misnomer when it comes to a college or university. Change isn't something that academic leaders manage. It's something that they lead, initiate, guide, and occasionally capture."[8]

Yes, it seems clear that there are multiple barriers and pressures that might distract or even stymie the hopes of a typical dean or director to instigate or support radical change if that change is being championed by her alone. Music leaders have no way of easily sidestepping the myriad pressures and challenges bearing down on higher education institutions, or of easily escaping the idiosyncrasies that make our higher education institutions resistant to change, or of easily discarding the culture that often makes our classical music area of study so wary of anything that would destabilize the centrality of such prized concepts as the formal concert and great works. And most of us—embedded as our music units might be within a larger university—have no way of radically changing a curriculum review process that remains better suited to the rate of societal and workplace change of the 1930s.

But if the need for change in our programs, in our curricula, and in our pedagogies is real, how do we move enable change on a large scale? How do we not only enable it to occur powerfully within our individual institutions but also enable innovative work to become diffused *among* the majority of our music departments and schools nationwide?[9]

In considering the advice that was shared by the higher education leaders, as outlined earlier, it's clear that our schools often contain leadership that develops (or sometimes intuits) strategies that can help a community to perceive a need for change, consider options, and, newly invested in a still stronger image of a desirable future and place of work, undertake the emotionally taxing work of pursuing serious change.

But we do not need to continue like this, with each music school and department trying to imagine a brighter future and each leader or group of leaders trying to invent a strategic path and collaborative process that might enable the needed change to occur. We have some significant opportunities, and none is perhaps more extraordinary (or more demanding of our collective courage and energy) than our moving to make a true and comprehensive investment in the people who can help realize the change and innovative that is needed. That means investing in the training of current *and* future leaders.

Whether through a consortium of higher education institutions or within organizations such as CMS, NASM, or National Association for Music Education (NAfME),[10] we could do much better in investing in the very people who can pursue and sustain the challenging work ahead, reorienting our classical music–related degrees to privilege a focus on those skills and areas of knowledge referenced in the previous two chapters. *Indeed, the argument could be made that we won't meet the challenges ahead without doing this foundational work.*

To be clear, our pursuit of the recommendations presented here would require a collective agreement among us in associations such as CMS or NASM that we have an obligation and a critical need to better prepare music students for the changing classical music marketplace and to further nudge our classical music culture toward being one that is more open, innovative, and authentic. If we were to reach that reasonable agreement, the pursuit of actions such as those recommended here would not be overly difficult. Each, after all, largely mirrors strategic initiatives already being utilized in one or more other disciplinary areas within academe.

Recommendations

1. *We could undertake a major initiative (co-sponsored by either a consortium of higher education institutions, or music organizations such as CMS, NASM, and NAfME, together with experts on leadership development and the higher education setting) to provide current, new, and emerging music program leaders across the country with a well-developed and highly focused professional development program around change leadership.*

Yes, care would be needed to ensure that we partner with leadership and adult development experts who are able to help ensure the delivery of leadership development training that is not only well grounded in change leadership and adult development theories but also deliberately oriented to navigate the values and peculiarities of nonprofit higher education organizations. But numerous such experts and helpful models exist. In terms of models, one immediately thinks of the year-long Academic Leadership Fellows Program run by the American Association of Colleges of Pharmacy (AACP) for current and emerging faculty leaders within that field.[11] That leadership program runs for a substantial time and features multiple touchpoints along the way. The presence of multiple touchpoints is likely critical. As leadership guru Barbara Kellerman has pointed out, for any leadership program to be impactful, it needs to be broad and multipronged and crafted with a clear understanding of the critical importance of (and the difference between) leadership education, leadership training, and leadership development.[12]

The investment needed for crafting such a nationwide opportunity for current and emergent faculty leaders would be sizable but would offer great promise. To a large extent, our future lies in the hands of current and potential leaders within our communities. We would be investing deeply in the future of classical music if we did better to strategically invest in them.

2. *We could make a more organized effort to strategically partner with the industry that will employ our graduates.*

Many higher education music programs and schools already have informal partnerships or relationships with regional professional arts organizations (whether performing ensembles, music industry companies, or arts presenters). By strengthening those partnerships further, our music schools and programs would help create internships and cooperative learning opportunities for students, providing them with much needed real-world experience and further understanding of career options and trajectories. Students' increased involvement in regional professional organizations would come with additional and mutual benefits; organizations could gain a much-needed youthful perspective on the experiences or products offered by the employing organization, and students could gain a firsthand understanding not only of further career options but of trends in the relationship between music-related products and services and the consumer public.

A related point deserves to be made here. Our music schools and programs would also do well to increase partnerships with nonmusic-related cultural organizations and with adjacent academic units in the sciences and health/medicine. Our students, after all, have much to gain from a broader and practical understanding of the place of music and music making in broader social contexts and areas of research. And classical music's future would be stronger for having a cadre of music advocates experienced in making connections between their music making and other aspects of society, work, and research.[13]

3. *Beyond the general leadership development program suggested in number 1, we (whether through a consortium of institutions, or through organizations such as CMS, NASM, or NAfME) could also partner with appropriate leadership development and cultural experts to develop and offer such leadership programs with a targeted focus on supporting and mentoring those leaders in our*

music programs and schools from underrepresented populations
(beginning with women and people of color).

There is no good reason remaining for us to keep starving our institutions of the energy and creative skill that would necessarily be present if we truly honored diversity and creativity and ensured strong opportunity for those underrepresented in our leadership pool to emerge. When it comes to gender, study after study has shown that women frequently demonstrate higher leadership performance than men in multiple leadership skill categories.[13] And the work of honoring racial and ethnic diversity is made only more pressing to those preoccupied with organizational effectiveness given such facts as the following: racial and ethnic diversity in business leadership is linked to greater financial returns, racially diverse teams produce better solutions to complex problems, and diversity in leadership and faculty helps with retention and success of diverse students and staff.[14] Will this work be easy? No. But as all of those who are not white and male have already revealed, power sharing is possible.

Closely related to these points is the additional opportunity we face to collectively reorient the job descriptions for our classical music area faculty to include special and privileged focus not only on such critical competencies as collaboration and innovation around audience engagement and development but also on evidence that candidates could further strengthen our community's commitment to diversity, equity, and inclusion.[15]

4. *Our schools could undertake a major initiative to reshape our DMA and PhD degrees to ensure that our graduating students exit with critical skills and knowledge related to innovation and change. And we could undertake further initiative to give greater space and support for doctoral students who are artists and scholars from underrepresented backgrounds (beginning with gender and race/ethnicity).*

This final recommendation is perhaps the most self-explanatory. Of special interest to our field might by the PhD Project, an initiative that has achieved unusual success in creating a powerful pipeline for African American, Latinx, and Native American academic faculty through business PhD programs.[16]

Final Reflection

The set of recommendations presented here is built on recognition that there is no singular solution to the interrelated puzzles and challenges we face. Rick Nason's work related to complexity and organizations was mentioned in the previous chapter. To reiterate, he admonishes that we should be careful to differentiate between complex problems (which he defines as problems that have solutions, for example, how to get an astronaut to the moon and back) and complicated issues that involve so many unknowns and so many interrelated factors that it is futile for us to try to shape a solution (e.g., raising a teenager or, we might add, addressing the challenges facing classical music and higher education). "Complex situations," he explained, "do not lend themselves to a solution, and it is folly to spend the time, energy, or effort even to attempt to create solutions."[17]

In making the recommendations we do, we are acknowledging that the changes we face in classical music and higher education together constitute *complicated issues*. By undertaking action that better equips our higher education music leaders to help others navigate the difficulties inherent in making large scale change of the type described in this monograph, we are making the most prudent of available investments. We are creating space and support for more widespread innovative, generous, and forward-oriented work.

The reader may have noticed two quotations at the front of this book. They are reprinted here.

> *A time of turbulence is a dangerous time, but its*
> *greatest danger is a temptation to deny reality*
>
> – Peter Drucker

> *We would rather be ruined than changed,*
> *We would rather die in our dread*
> *Than climb the cross of the moment*
> *And let our illusions die.*
>
> – W. H. Auden

It is clear that we have long been tempted to deny the reality of both a changed marketplace and the resulting need for a complete reimagining of our performance-training model. It is similarly clear that we have an intrinsic aversion to pursue (and undergo) the significant change that such a reimagined training model demands of ourselves and our work.

In recognizing both of these things, we can further appreciate why our collective and broad investment in the development of skilled leaders is so important. Simply put, we will need some heroic mentoring and encouragement to do the work that lies in front of us.

Notes

1. The recommendation that hiring be done with an eye to giving creative faculty space to do innovative work aligns perfectly with the contention in the previous chapter that we can do better to provide students with space and support to lead.
2. It must be acknowledged that the higher education leaders who participated in this study include only individuals who are well positioned professionally and who have had a markedly successful career compared to many of their peers. Given that, it is safe to assume they not only have an unusually strong skill set as leaders but also have a sense of confidence that may be beyond the norm.
3. Readers who wish to gain a fuller introduction to change management models and theories are encouraged to consult such works as the following: R. Mauborgne, W. C. Kim, and J. P. Kotter, *HBR's 10 Must Reads on Change Management* (Boston, MA: Harvard Business Review Press, 2011), and E. Cameron and M. Green, *Making Sense of Change Management: A Complete Guide to the Models, Tools and Techniques of Organizational Change* (Philadelphia, PA: Kogan Page, 2015).
4. One of the most famous (and neatest) of change management models remains the three-stage or three-step model originally developed and introduced by Kurt Lewin in the late 1940s and the early 1950s. A model that sought to both illuminate the dynamics involved in change as well as the leadership that might be appropriate to manage that change, Lewin's change model illuminated three essential steps or stages—"Unfreeze" (preparation for change); "Change" (the stage of change or transition); and "Refreeze" (the stage when the change has been implemented and accepted, and the organization is again becoming stable). See especially K. Lewin, *Field Theory in Social Science* (New York: Harper and Row, 1951). See also K. Lewin, "Frontiers in Group Dynamics: Concept, Method and Reality in Social Science: Social Equilibria and Social Change," *Human Relations* 1, no. 1 (1947): 5–41, doi: 10.1177/001872674700100103, accessed February 21, 2019; K. Lewin, "Group Decision and Social Change," in *Readings in Social Psychology*, edited by T. M. Newcomb and E. L. Hartley (New York: Henry Holt, 1947), 330–344. For an especially thorough analysis of Lewin's threefold concept of change (and its historical reception), see S. Cummings, T. Bridgman, and K. G. Brown, "Unfreezing Change as Three Steps: Rethinking Kurt Lewin's Legacy for Change Management," *Human Relations* 69, no. 1 (2015): 33–60, doi: 10.1177/0018726715577707, accessed February 21, 2019.
5. Few change management models and theories have been more widely discussed in business and management literature than John Kotter's eight-stage model of effective change management. Built from a careful analysis of leadership over change efforts that were unsuccessful and those that

were successful, Kotter's model (first outlined in 1995 and developed in subsequent years) has spawned an entire industry. Resources are available through his organization's website, www.kotterinc.com/, his main writings are as follows (organized chronologically): J. P. Kotter, "Leading Change: Why Transformation Efforts Fail," *Harvard Business Review*, May 1995, https://hbr.org/1995/05/leading-change-why-transformation-efforts-fail-2, accessed February 21, 2019; J. P. Kotter, "Winning at Change," *Leader to Leader* no. 10 (1998): 27–33, doi: 10.1002/ltl.40619981009, accessed February 21, 2019; J. P. Kotter and H. Rathgeber, *Our Iceberg Is Melting: Changing and Succeeding Under Any Conditions* (New York: St. Martin's Press, 2006); J. P. Kotter, *A Sense of Urgency* (Boston, MA: Harvard Business Press, 2008); J. P. Kotter, *Leading Change* (Boston, MA: Harvard Business Review Press, 2012).

6. Though it is presented as the stages that individuals typically go through when they are confronted with news of a terminal illness, the model that Swiss-American Elisabeth Kübler-Ross developed a has become increasingly employed as a way of understanding how people (whether individually or within groups) deal with prospects of difficult change (which typically include expectations and feelings of loss). Kübler-Ross's model was outlined formally in her book, *On Death and Dying* (New York: Macmillan, 1969). Her model has been adapted variously into models around organizational change. See, for example, T. R. Harvey and L. B. Wehmeyer, *Checklist for Change: A Pragmatic Approach to Creating and Controlling Change* (Boston, MA: Allyn and Bacon, 1990).

7. Higher education leader and noted Canadian education theorist Michael Fullan developed this model after investigating change dynamics within both educational and business settings. His theories and arguments have drawn special praise for their contention that change is messy and that the presence of these leadership traits simply strengthens the chance for success within organizations where change is being pursued. Fullan's model is outlined and presented in various forms in his core works: M. Fullan, *Understanding Change: Leading in a Culture of Change* (San Francisco, CA: Jossey-Bass, 2001); M. Fullan, *Change Leader: Learning to Do What Matters Most* (Hoboken, NJ: Wiley & Sons, 2011); M. Fullan, *Leading in a Culture of Change* (Hoboken, NJ: Wiley & Sons, 2014); M. Fullan, *The New Meaning of Educational Change* (New York: Teachers College Press, 2016). See also his website, https://michaelfullan.ca/.

8. J. L. Buller, *Change Leadership in Higher Education: A Practical Guide to Academic Transformation* (Hoboken, NJ: John Wiley & Sons, 2014), 24.

9. While the list of recommendations is made independent of any sources, Rogers's volume on innovations and their diffusion and adopted was of value in spurring thinking. See E. M. Rogers, *The Diffusion of Innovations*, 5th ed. (New York: Free Press, 2013).

10. NAfME certainly should be included in this conversation and work. After all, one of its core constituent groups—the teachers of undergraduates enrolled in music education degrees—will disproportionally end up shaping the expectations and values of many children who will become undergraduate music students, whether in music performance or music education. In that way, it is significantly impacting the values of the very individuals who will become future faculty within music programs and music schools.

11. American Association of Colleges of Pharmacy, Academic Leadership Fellows Program. See www.aacp.org/resource/academic-leadership-fellows-program, accessed February 12, 2019.

12. Kellerman is not only a leading expert on leadership studies but also a longtime skeptic of leadership training. Her criticisms have long been formidable and helpful. In her most recent book, she draws attention to the distinct and important role of three strategies to strengthen leadership: educating potential leaders; training for leadership; and developing leaders over time. See B. Kellerman, *Professionalizing Leadership* (New York: Oxford University Press, 2018).

13. As researchers Zenger and Folkman learned from their extensive review of leadership evaluations, women were more highly rated than men in fully 12 of the 16 competencies that go into outstanding leadership. J. Zenger and J. Folkman, "Are Women Better Leaders Than Men?," *Harvard Business Review*, March 15, 2012, https://hbr.org/2012/03/a-study-in-leadership-women-do, accessed February 21, 2019. For additional confirmation of women outperforming men in leadership skills and categories, see L. A. Pfaff, K. J. Boatwright, A. L. Potthoff, C. Finan, L. A. Ulrey, and D. M. Huber, "Perceptions of Women and Men Leaders Following 360-Degree Feedback Evaluations," *Performance Improvement Quarterly* 26, no. 1 (2013): 35–56, doi: 10.1002/piq.21134, accessed February 21, 2019. See also H. Ibarra, D. Tannen, and J. C. Williams, *HBR's 10 Must Reads on Women and Leadership* (Watertown, MA: Harvard Business Review, 2018). Also see J. M. Ruiz-Jiménez, M. Fuentes-Fuentes, and M. Ruiz-Arroyo, "Knowledge Combination Capability and Innovation: The Effects of Gender Diversity on Top Management Teams in Technology-Based Firms," *Journal of Business Ethics* 135, no. 3 (May 2016): 503–515, doi: 10.1007/s10551-014-2462-7, accessed February 21, 2019. For a general introduction to related literature see "Why Diversity Matters," *Catalyst Information Center*, July 2012, www.catalyst.org/system/files/why_diversity_matters_catalyst.pdf, accessed February 19, 2019.

14. As a carefully researched report put out by McKinsey & Company recently affirmed, "companies in the top-quartile for ethnic/cultural diversity on executive teams were 33% more likely to have industry-leading profitability." V. Hunt, S. Prince, S. Dixon-Fyle, and L. Yee, *Delivering Through Diversity*, McKinsey & Company, January 2018, 1, www.mckinsey.com/~/media/McKinsey/Business%20Functions/Organization/Our%20Insights/Delivering%20through%20diversity/Delivering-through-diversity_full-report.ashx. See also S. A. Hewlett, M. Marshall, and L. Sherbin, "How Diversity Can Drive Innovation," *Harvard Business Review*, December 2013, https://hbr.org/2013/12/how-diversity-can-drive-innovation, accessed February 21, 2019; D. G. Smith and N. B. Schonfeld, "The Benefits of Diversity: What the Research Tells Us," *About Campus* 5, no. 5 (November 1, 2000): 16–23, doi: 10.1177/108648220000500505, accessed February 21, 2019; S. Kerby and C. Burns, "The Top 10 Economic Facts of Diversity in the Workplace: A Diverse Workforce Is Integral to a Strong Economy," *Center for American Progress*, July 12, 2012, https://cdn.americanprogress.org/wp-content/uploads/issues/2012/07/pdf/diverse_workplace.pdf, accessed February 21, 2019. And see K. Phillips, "How Diversity Makes Us Smarter: Being Around People Who Are Different

From Us Makes Us More Creative, More Diligent and Harder-Working," *Scientific American* 331, no. 4 (October 1, 2014): 42–47, doi: 10.1038/scientificamerican1014-42, accessed February 21, 2019. We have access to many methods of doing better in diversity hiring and clear affirmation of the myths that have for too long stymied advances in this field within the academy. L. Dietz, P. Fain, S. Jaschik, R. Seltzer, J. Logue, J. New, and E. Wexler, "Recruitment, Diversity and Success," *Inside Higher Ed*, 2016, https://q8rkuwu1ti4vaqw33x41zocd-wpengine.netdna-ssl.com/conservatory/files/2018/09/Recruitment-Diversity-Success.pdf, accessed February 12, 2019; D. G. Smith and J. F. Moreno, "Hiring the Next Generation of Professors: Will Myths Remain Excuses?," *Chronicle of Higher Education* 53, no. 6, https://q8rkuwu1ti4vaqw33x41zocd-wpengine.netdna-ssl.com/conservatory/files/2018/09/Hiring-the-Next-Generation-of-Professors-The-Chronicle-of-Higher-Education.pdf accessed February 12, 2019; *Diversity and Faculty Recruitment: Myths and Realities*, Office for Faculty Equity and Welfare, University of California, Berkeley, 2018.

15. Many institutions have begun to include such specific language in all faculty job descriptions. Here is the one now adopted and used at Shenandoah University: "Applicants should note that Shenandoah University is committed to enriching its educational experience and culture through the diversity of its faculty, administration, and staff. *All candidates are strongly encouraged to include a statement in their cover letters addressing ways in which they may be able to contribute to that commitment.*"

16. To learn more about The PhD Project, please see their main website at www.phdproject.org/. Though a little dated, a more general overview of efforts nationwide around pipeline projects that strengthen the diversity of doctoral programs is found in the following report: "Diversity & the Ph.D.," *Woodrow Wilson National Fellowship Foundation*, 2005, www.uky.edu/ie/sites/www.uky.edu.ie/files/uploads/Diversity%20%26%20the%20PhD%20A%20Review%20of%20Efforts%20to%20Broaden%20Race%20%26%20Ethnicity%20.%20.%20.pdf, accessed February 12, 2019.

17. See R. Nason, *It's Not Complicated: The Art and Science of Complexity in Business* (Toronto: University of Toronto Press, 2017), 94.

Bibliography

"About the PHD Project." *The PHD Project*, Accessed April 6, 2019. www.phdproject.org/.

"Academic Leadership Fellows Program." *American Association of Colleges of Pharmacy*, Accessed April 6, 2019. www.aacp.org/resource/academic-leadership-fellows-program.

Berkeley Office for Faculty Equity and Welfare. *Diversity and Faculty Recruitment: Myths and Realities*. Report. Office for Faculty Equity and Welfare, University of California, Berkeley. Berkeley, CA: UC Berkeley, 2018.

Buller, J.L. *Change Leadership in Higher Education: A Practical Guide to Academic Transformation*. Hoboken, NJ: John Wiley & Sons, Incorporated, 2014.

Cameron, E. and M. Green. *Making Sense of Change Management: A Complete Guide to the Models, Tools and Techniques of Organizational Change.* Philadelphia, PA: Kogan Page, 2015.

Cummings, S., T. Bridgman, and K.G. Brown. "Unfreezing Change as Three Steps: Rethinking Kurt Lewin's Legacy for Change Management." *Human Relations* 69, no. 1 (2015): 33–60.

Dietz, L., P. Fain, S. Jaschik, R. Seltzer, J. Logue, J. New, and E. Wexler. "Recruitment, Diversity and Success." *Inside Higher Ed*, 2016. Accessed February 12, 2019. https://q8rkuwu1ti4vaqw33x41zocd-wpengine.netdna-ssl.com/conservatory/files/2018/09/Recruitment-Diversity-Success.pdf.

"Diversity & the Ph.D." The Woodrow Wilson National Fellowship Foundation, May, 2005. Accessed February 12, 2019. www.uky.edu/ie/sites/www.uky.edu.ie/files/uploads/Diversity%20%26%20the%20PhD%20A%20Review%20of%20Efforts%20to%20Broaden%20Race%20%26%20Ethnicity%20.%20.%20.pdf.

Fullan, M. *Change Leader: Learning to Do What Matters Most.* Hoboken, NJ: John Wiley & Sons, Incorporated, 2011.

Fullan, M. *Leading in a Culture of Change.* Hoboken, NJ: John Wiley & Sons, Incorporated, 2014.

Fullan, M. "Michael Fullan: Author, Speaker, Educational Consultant." *Michael Fullan.* Accessed February 21, 2019. https://michaelfullan.ca/.

Fullan, M. *The New Meaning of Educational Change.* New York, NY: Teachers College Press, 2016.

Fullan, M. *Understanding Change: Leading in a Culture of Change.* San Francisco, CA: Jossey-Bass, 2001.

Harvey, T.R. and L.B. Wehmeyer. *Checklist for Change: A Pragmatic Approach to Creating and Controlling Change.* Boston, MA: Allyn and Bacon, 1990.

Hewlett, S.A., Marshall, M., and Sherbin, L. "How Diversity Can Drive Innovation." *Harvard Business Review*, December, 2013. Accessed February 21, 2019. https://hbr.org/2013/12/how-diversity-can-drive-innovation.

Hunt, V., S. Prince, S. Dixon-Fyle, and L. Yee. *Delivering through Diversity.* Report. McKinsey & Company. New York, NY: McKinsey, 2018. www.mckinsey.com/~/media/McKinsey/Business%20Functions/Organization/Our%20Insights/Delivering%20through%20diversity/Delivering-through-diversity_full-report.ashx.

Ibarra, H., D. Tannen, and J.C. Williams. *HBR's 10 Must Reads on Women and Leadership.* Watertown, MA: Harvard Business Review, 2018.

Kellerman, B. *Professionalizing Leadership.* New York, NY: Oxford University Press, 2018.

Kerby, S. and C. Burns. "The Top 10 Economic Facts of Diversity in the Workplace: A Diverse Workforce Is Integral to a Strong Economy." *Center for American Progress*, July 12, 2012. Accessed February 21, 2019. https://cdn.americanprogress.org/wp-content/uploads/issues/2012/07/pdf/diverse_workplace.pdf.

Kotter, J.P. *Leading Change.* Boston, MA: Harvard Business Review Press, 2012.

Kotter, J.P. "Leading Change: Why Transformation Efforts Fail." *Harvard Business Review*, May, 1995. Accessed February 21, 2019. https://hbr.org/1995/05/leading-change-why-transformation-efforts-fail-2.

Kotter, J.P. *A Sense of Urgency*. Boston, MA: Harvard Business Press, 2008.

Kotter, J.P. "Together, So Much More Is Possible." *Kotter*. Accessed February 21, 2019. www.kotterinc.com/.

Kotter, J.P. "Winning at Change." *Leader to Leader* no. 10 (1998): 27–33.

Kotter, J.P. and H. Rathgeber. *Our Iceberg Is Melting: Changing and Succeeding Under Any Conditions*. New York, NY: St. Martin's Press, 2006.

Kübler-Ross, E. *On Death and Dying*. New York, NY: Macmillan Company, 1969.

Lewin, K. *Field Theory in Social Science*. New York, NY: Harper and Row, 1951.

Lewin, K. "Frontiers in Group Dynamics: Concept, Method and Reality in Social Science; Social Equilibria and Social Change." *Human Relations* 1, no. 1 (1947): 5–41.

Lewin, K. "Group Decision and Social Change." In *Readings in Social Psychology*, ed. T.M. Newcomb and E.L. Hartley, 330–344. New York, NY: Henry Holt, 1947.

Mauborgne, R., W.C. Kim, and J.P. Kotter. *HBR's 10 Must Reads on Change Management*. Boston, MA: Harvard Business Review Press, 2011.

Nason, R. *It's Not Complicated: The Art and Science of Complexity in Business*. Toronto, Canada: University of Toronto Press, 2017.

Pfaff, L.A., K.J. Boatwright, A.L. Potthoff, C. Finan, L.A. Ulrey, and D.M. Huber. "Perceptions of Women and Men Leaders Following 360-Degree Feedback Evaluations." *Performance Improvement Quarterly* 26, no. 1 (2013): 35–56.

Phillips, K. "How Diversity Makes Us Smarter: Being Around People Who Are Different from Us Makes Us More Creative, More Diligent and Harder-Working." *Scientific American* 331, no. 4 (2014): 42–47.

Rogers, E.M. *The Diffusion of Innovations* (5th ed.). New York, NY: Free Press, 2013.

Ruiz-Jiménez, J.M., M. Fuentes-Fuentes, and M. Ruiz-Arroyo. "Knowledge Combination Capability and Innovation: The Effects of Gender Diversity on Top Management Teams in Technology-Based Firms." *Journal of Business Ethics* 135 no. 3 (2016): 503–515.

Smith, D.G. and J.F. Moreno. "Hiring the Next Generation of Professors: Will Myths Remain Excuses?" *The Chronicle of Higher Education* 53, no. 6 (2006). Accessed February 12, 2019. https://q8rkuwu1ti4vaqw33x41zocd-wpengine.netdna-ssl.com/conservatory/files/2018/09/Hiring-the-Next-Generation-of-Professors-The-Chronicle-of-Higher-Education.pdf.

Smith, D.G. and N.B. Schonfeld. "The Benefits of Diversity What the Research Tells Us." *About Campus* 5, no. 5 (2000): 16–23.

"Why Diversity Matters." *Catalyst Information Center*, July, 2012. Accessed February 19, 2019. www.catalyst.org/system/files/why_diversity_matters_catalyst.pdf.

Zenger, J. and J. Folkman. "Are Women Better Leaders Than Men?" *Harvard Business Review*, March 15, 2012. Accessed February 21, 2019. https://hbr.org/2012/03/a-study-in-leadership-women-do.

Appendix
Select Readings on Leadership, and Leading Change in Higher Education

Aguirre, A., Martinez, R.O., and Association for the Study of Higher Education. (2006). *Diversity leadership in higher education*. Ashe Higher Education Report, V. 32, No. 3. San Francisco: Jossey-Bass.

Altbach, P.G., Berdahl, R.O., and Gumport, P.J. (1994). *Higher education in American Society* (3rd ed.). Amherst, NY: Prometheus Books.

Anderson, J.A. (2008). *Driving change through diversity and globalization: Transformative leadership in the academy*. Sterling, VA: Stylus Publishing.

Barnett, R. (2004). Learning for an unknown future. *Higher Education Research & Development*, 23(3), 247–260.

Bastedo, M.N., Altbach, P.G., and Gumport, P.J. (2016). *American higher education in the twenty-first century: Social, political, and economic challenges* (4th ed.). Baltimore: Johns Hopkins University Press.

Becher, T. and Trowler, P.R. (2001). *Academic tribes and territories* (2nd ed. repr.). Philadelphia, PA: Open University Press.

Berry, J. (2005). *Reclaiming the ivory towers: Organizing adjuncts to change higher education*. New York, NY: Monthly Review Press.

Bolden, R., Jones, S., Davis, H., and Gentle, P. (2015). *Developing and sustaining shared leadership in higher education*. Stimulus Paper Series of the Leadership Foundation for Higher Education. London: Leadership Foundation for Higher Education and L. H. Martin Institute.

Bolman, L.G. and Gallos, J.V. (2011). *Reframing academic leadership*. San Francisco, CA: Jossey-Bass.

Brown, S. (2002). Re-engineering the university. *Open Learning*, 17(3), 231–243.

Brown-Glaude, W.R. (2009). *Doing diversity in higher education: Faculty leaders share challenges and strategies*. New Brunswick, NJ: Rutgers University Press.

Bryman, A. (2009). *Effective leadership in higher education: Summary of findings*. Research and Development Series. London: Leadership Foundation for Higher Education.

Buchan, J.F. (2011). The chicken or the egg? Investigating the transformational impact of learning technology. *Research in Learning Technology*, 19(2), 155–172.

Buller, J.L. (2014). Change leadership for chairs. *Department Chair*, 24(3), 3–5.

Buller, J.L. (2015). *Change leadership in higher education: A practical guide to academic transformation.* San Francisco, CA: Jossey-Bass.

Chesterton, P., Duignan, P., Felton, E., Flowers, K., Gibbons, P., Horne, M., and Koop, T. (2008). *Development of distributed institutional leadership capacity in online learning and teaching project.* Final Report. Australian Learning and Teaching Council. Retrieved from www.olt.gov.au/resource.

Christensen, C.M. and Eyring, H.J. (2011). *The innovative university: Changing the DNA of higher education from the inside out.* San Francisco, CA: Jossey-Bass.

Christensen, C.M., Horn, M.B., Caldera, L., and Soares, L. (2011). *Disrupting college: How disruptive innovation can deliver quality and affordability to postsecondary education.* Center for American Progress and Insight Institute.

Clark, B.R. (2007). *Sustaining change in universities.* Maidenhead: McGraw Hill International.

Coaldrake, P. and Stedman, L. (1998). *On the brink: Australia's universities confronting their future.* St Lucia, Brisbane: University of Queensland Press.

Cohen, P. (2004). The crisis of the university. *Campus Review*, April 21–27, 9–12.

Cooper, T. (2002). *Concepts of "quality": And the problem of "customers," "products," and purpose in higher education.* Proceedings of HERDSA Annual Conference, pp. 144–151.

Cranston, N., Ehrich, L.C., and Kimber, M. (2006). Ethical dilemmas: The "bread and butter" of educational leaders' lives. *Journal of Educational Administration*, 44(2), 106–119.

Cuban, L. (2001). *Oversold and underused: Computers in the classroom.* Cambridge, MA: Harvard University Press.

D'Ambrosio, M. and Ehrenberg, R.G. (2007). *Transformational change in higher education: Positioning colleges and universes or future success.* Cheltenham, UK: Edward Elgar.

Davies, B. (2003). Death to critique and dissent? The policies and practices of new managerialism and of "evidence-based practice". *Gender and Education*, 15(1), 91–103. doi:10.1080/0954025032000042167.

Davis, H. and Jones, S. (2014). The work of leadership in higher education management. *Journal of Higher Education Policy and Management*, 36(4), 367–370. doi:10.1080/1360080X.2014.916463.

Dearlove, J. (1997). The academic labour process: From collegiality and professionalism to managerialism and proletarianism? *The Higher Education Review*, 1, 56.

Deem, R. (1998). "New managerialism" and higher education: The management of performance and cultures in universities in the United Kingdom. *International Studies in Sociology of Education*, 8(1), 47–70. doi:10.1080/0962021980020014.

Dempster, N. and Berry, V. (2003). Blindfolded in a minefield: Principals' ethical decision-making. *Cambridge Journal of Education*, 33(3), 457–477.

Diamond, R.M. (2006). Why colleges are so hard to change. *Inside Higher Ed*, September 8. Retrieved from www.insidehighered.com/views/2006/09/08/why-colleges-are-so-hard-change.

Dopson, S., Ferlie, E., McGivern, G., Fischer, M., Ledger, J., Behrens, S., and Wilson, S. (2016). *The impact of leadership and leadership development in higher education: A review of the literature and evidence*. Research and Development Series of the Leadership Foundation for Higher Education. London: Leadership Foundation for Higher Education.

Drew, G. (2006). Balancing academic advancement with business effectiveness? The dual role for senior university leaders. *The International Journal of Knowledge, Culture and Organisational Change*, 6(4), 117–125.

Drew, G., Ehrich, L.C., and Hansford, B.C. (2008). An exploration of university leaders' perceptions of leadership and learning. *Leading & Managing*, 14(2), 1–18.

European Union. (2015). *The changing pedagogical landscape: New ways of teaching and learning and their implications for higher education policy*. Directorate-General for Education and Culture, European Commission, written by Jeff Haywood, Louise Connelly, Piet Henderikx, Martin Weller, Keith Williams, Luxembourg, Publications Office at the European Union. Retrieved July 9, 2018, from https://publications.europa.eu/en/publication-detail/-/publication/f43a8447-7948-11e5-86db01aa75ed71a1.

Evans, C. and Kozhevnikov, M. (Eds.). (2013). *Styles of practice in higher education: Exploring approaches to teaching and learning*. Florence, KY: Taylor & Francis.

Figlio, D.N., Schapiro, M.O., and Soter, K.B. (2013). *Are tenure track professors better teachers?* National Bureau of Economic Research Working Paper No. 19406.

Fitch, P. and Van Brunt, B. (2016). *A guide to leadership and management in higher education: Managing across the generations*. New York, NY: Routledge.

Fletcher, J. and Kaufer, K. (2003). Shared leadership: Paradox and possibilities. In C. Pearce and J. Conger (Eds.), *Shared leadership: Reframing the hows and whys of leadership* (pp. 21–47). Thousand Oaks, CA: Sage Publications.

Fullan, M. (1993). *Change forces: Probing the depths of educational reform*. School Development and the Management of Change Series, 10. Bristol, PA: Falmer Press.

Fullan, M. (2001). *The new meaning of educational change*. New York, NY: Teachers College Press.

Fullan, M. (2002). The change leader. *Beyond Instructional Leadership*, May, 59(8), 16–21.

Gayle, D.J., Tewarie, A.B., and White, A.Q. (2003a). *Governance in 21st century universities*. San Francisco, CA: Jossey-Bass.

Gayle, D.J., Tewarie, A.B., and White, A.Q., Jr. (2003b). Governance in the twenty-first century university: Approaches to effective leadership and strategic management. *ASHE-ERIC Higher Education Report*, 30(1).

Gentle, P. and Forman, D. (2014). *Engaging leaders: The challenge of inspiring collective commitment in universities*. London: Routledge.

Giroux, H. (2005). Academic entrepreneurs: The corporate takeover of higher education. *Tikkun*, 20(2), 18–28.

Govindarajan, V. and Trimble, C. (2010). *The other side of innovation: Solving the execution challenge*. Boston, MA: Harvard Business School Press.

Green, W. and Ruutz, A. (2008). *Fit for purpose: Designing a faculty-based community of (teaching) practice, in Engaging Communities*. Proceedings of the 31st HERDSA Annual Conference, Rotorua, 1–4 July, pp. 163–172.

Gronn, P. (2000). Distributed properties. *Educational Management & Administration*, 28(3), 317–338.

Gunn, C. (2010). Sustainability factors for e-learning initiatives. *ALT-J: Research in Learning Technology*, 18(2), 89–103.

Hargreaves, A., Fink, D., and Harris, A. (2008). Distributed leadership: Democracy or delivery? *Journal of Educational Administration*, 46(2), 229–240.

Hargreaves, A. and Shirley, D. (2009). The three ways of change. In A. Hargreaves and D. Shirley (Eds.), *The fourth way: The inspiring future for educational change* (pp. 1–19). Thousand Oaks, CA: Corwin Press.

Harris, A. (2004). Teacher leadership and distributed leadership: An exploration of the literature. *Leading and Managing*, 10(2), 1–9.

Harris, A. (2008a). Distributed leadership: According to the evidence. *Journal of Educational Administration*, 46(2), 172–188.

Harris, A. (2008b). *Distributed school leadership: Developing tomorrow's leaders*. London: Routledge.

Hartley, D. (2007). The emergence of distributed leadership in education: Why now? *British Journal of Education Studies*, 55(2), 202–214.

Hartley, D. (2016). Economic crisis, technology and the management of education: The case of distributed leadership. *Educational Management Administration & Leadership*, 44(2), 173–183.

Harvey, M. (2008). *Leadership and assessment: Strengthening the nexus*. Final Report. Strawberry Hills and Australian Learning and Teaching Council. Retrieved from www.olt.gov.au/ resource?text=Harvey.

Haywood, J. (2015). Might MOOCs still be disruptive? In *The Europa world of learning 2016* (pp. 14–20). Abingdon: Routledge.

Haywood, J. and Macleod, H. (2014). To MOOC or not to MOOC? University decision-making and agile governance for educational innovation. In K. Paul (Ed.), *Massive open online courses: The MOOC revolution* (pp. 46–60). New York, NY: Routledge.

Haywood, J., Woodgate, A., and Dewhurst, D. (2015). Reflections of an early MOOC provider: Achievements and future directions. In C.J. Bonk, M.M. Lee, T.C. Reeves, and T.H. Reynolds (Eds.), *Open education around the world* (pp. 89–102). New York, NY: Routledge.

HBR-Harvard Business Review (2011). *HBR's 10 must reads on leadership*. Boston, MA: Harvard Business Review Press.

Hendrickson, R.M., Lane, J.E., Harris, J.T., and Dorman, R.H. (2013). *Academic leadership and governance of higher education: A guide for trustees, leaders, and aspiring leaders of two- and four-year institutions.* First. Sterling, VA: Stylus Publishing.

Higher Education Transformation Work Group. (2001). *Change and transformation in higher education: An annotated bibliography* (2nd ed.). Ann Arbor, MI: University of Michigan. Retrieved from https://pdfs.semanticscholar.org/8aa1/8ca93307bb1915e2c97b88d0f10449463b72.pdf.

Horn, M. (2014). *Beyond good and evil: Understanding the role of for-profits in education through the theories of disruptive innovation.* American Enterprise Institute. Institute-Wide Task Force on the Future of MIT Undergraduate Education: Final Report. Retrieved from http://web.mit.edu/future-report/TaskForceFinal_July28.pdf.

Jones, D.G. (2011). Academic leadership and departmental headship in turbulent times. *Tertiary Education and Management*, 17(4), 279–288.

Jones, S., Harvey, M., and Lefoe, G. (2014). A conceptual approach for blended leadership for tertiary education institutions. *Journal of Higher Education Policy and Management*, 36(4), 418–429.

Kellerman, B. (2004). *Bad leadership: What it is, how it happens, why it matters.* Boston, MA: Harvard Business School Press.

Kellerman, B. (2008). *Followership: How followers are creating change and changing leaders.* Boston, MA: Harvard Business Press.

Kellerman, B. (2012). *The end of leadership* (1st ed.). New York, NY: Harper Business Press.

Kellerman, B. (2018). *Professionalizing leadership.* New York, NY: Oxford University Press.

Keppel, M., O'Dwyer, C., Lyon, B., and Childs, M. (2010). Transforming distance education curricula through distributive leadership. *ALT-J: Research in Learning Technology*, 18(3), 165–178.

Kezar, A.J. (2014). *How colleges change: Understanding, leading, and enacting change.* New York, NY: Routledge.

Kotter, J.P. (1996). *Leading change.* Boston, MA: Harvard Business School Press.

Krull, W. (2012). Who is leading whom, where to, what for: And how? Governance and empowerment in the university of the twenty-first century. In A. Altmann and B. Ebersberger (Eds.), *Universities in change: Innovation, technology, and knowledge management* (pp. 117–133). New York, NY: Springer.

Lawrence, F.L. (2006). *Leadership in higher education: Views from the presidency.* New Brunswick, NJ: Transaction.

Lefoe, G. and Parrish, D. (2013). Changing culture: Developing a framework for leadership capacity development. In D.J. Salter (Eds.), *Cases on quality teaching practices in higher education* (pp. 239–260). Hershey, PA: IGI Global.

León, D.J. (2005). *Lessons in leadership: Executive leadership programs for advancing diversity in higher education.* Diversity in Higher Education, 5. Amsterdam: Elsevier JAI.

Longden, B. (2006). An institutional response to changing student expectations and their impact on retention rates. *Journal of Higher Education Policy and Management*, 28(2), 173–187.

Longman, K. and Madsen, S.R. (2014). *Women and leadership in higher education*. Women and Leadership: Research, Theory, and Practice. Charlotte, NC: Information Age Publishing.

Lumby, J. (2013). Distributed leadership: The use and abuses of power. *Educational Management and Leadership*, 41(5), 58–598.

Lumby, J. (2018). Leadership and power in higher education. *Studies in Higher Education*, 1–11.

MacFarlane, B. (2007). *The academic citizen*. London and New York, NY: Routledge.

Marshall, S.J. (2006). *Issues in the development of leadership for learning and teaching in higher education*. Report to Australian Learning and Teaching Council. Retrieved from www.olt.edu.au/resource.

Marshall, S.J. (2007). *Strategic leadership of change in higher education*. London: Routledge.

Marshall, S.J. (2010). Change, technology and higher education: Are universities capable of organisational change? *ALT-J: Research in Learning Technology*, 18(3), 179–192.

Marshall, S.J., Adams, M.J., Cameron, A., and Sullivan, G. (2000). Academics' perceptions of their professional development needs related to leadership and management: What can we learn? *International Journal for Academic Development*, 5(1), 42–53.

McKay, A. (2018). *The future of higher education in the United States*. Unpublished whitepaper. Shenandoah University, August 1.

McMurray, D.W. (2001). The importance of "goodness of fit" between organisational culture and climate in the management of change: A case study in the development of online learning. *ALT-J: Research in Learning Technology*, 9(1), 73–83.

Mead, P., Morgan, M., and Heath, C. (1999). Equipping leaders to capitalise on the outcomes of quality assessment in higher education. *Assessment and Evaluation in Higher Education*, 24(2), 147–156.

Meek, V.L. and Wood, F.Q. (1997). *Higher education government and management: An Australian study*. Evaluations and Investigations Program, Higher Education Division, Department of Employment, Education, Training and Youth Affairs, January. Retrieved September 13, 2003, from www.detya.gov.au/archive/highered/eippubs/eip9701/front.htm.

Middlehurst, R. (2007). The challenging journey: From leadership course to leadership foundation for higher education. *New Directions for Higher Education*, 137, 45–57.

Middlehurst, R. (2013). Changing internal governance: Are leadership roles and management structures in United Kingdom universities fit for the future? *Higher Education Quarterly*, 67(3), 275–294.

Mihalache, O.R., Jansen, J.J.P., Van den Bosch, F.A., and Volberda, H.W. (2014). Top management team, shared leadership and organizational ambidexterity: A moderated mediation framework. *Strategic Entrepreneurship Journal*, 8, 128–148.

Minthorn, R.S. and Chavez, A.F. (Eds.). (2016). *Indigenous leadership in higher education*. London: Routledge.

Newman, F., Couturier, L., and Scurry, J. (2004). *The future of higher education: Rhetoric, reality, and the risks of the market.* San Francisco, CA: Jossey-Bass.

Nixon, J. (1996). Professional identity and the restructuring of higher education. *Studies in Higher Education,* 21(1), 5–16.

Oliver, R. (2005). Ten more years of educational technologies in education: How far have we travelled? *Australian Educational Computing,* 20(1), 18–23.

Page, S.E. (2007). *The difference: How the power of diversity creates better groups, firms, schools, and societies.* Princeton, NJ: Princeton University Press.

Ramsden, P. (1998a). *Learning to lead in higher education.* London: Routledge.

Ramsden, P. (1998b). Managing the effective university. *Higher Education Research and Development,* 17(3), 347–370.

Randall, L. (2012). Transforming a university: A study of process leadership. *Academy of Educational Leadership Journal,* 16(2).

Rizvi, S., Donnelly, K., and Barber, M. (2013). *An avalanche is coming: Higher education and the revolution ahead.* London: Institute for Public Policy Research. Retrieved March 2018, from www.ippr.org/publications/an-avalanche-is-coming-higher-education-and-the-revolution-ahead.

Roche, V. (2001). Professional development models and transformative change: A case study of indicators of effective practice in higher education. *The International Journal for Academic Development,* 6(2), 121–129.

Rochford, F. (2006). Is there any clear idea of a university. *Journal of Higher Education Policy and Management,* 28(2), 147–158.

Rogers, E.M. (2013). *The diffusion of innovations* (5th ed.). New York, NY: Free Press.

Rowley, D.J., Lujan, H.D., and Dolence, M.G. (2001). *Strategic change in colleges and universities: Planning to survive and prosper.* San Francisco, CA: Jossey-Bass.

Ruben, B.D. and De Lisi, R. (2017). *A guide for leaders in higher education: Core concepts, competencies, and tools.* First. Sterling, VA: Stylus Publishing.

Santamaría, L.J. and Santamaría, A.P. (Eds.). (2016). *Culturally responsive leadership in higher education: Promoting access, equity, and improvement.* New York, NY: Routledge and Taylor & Francis.

Scott, G., Coates, H., and Anderson, M. (2008a). *Academic leadership capacities for Australian higher education.* Final Report to Australian Learning and Teaching Council. Retrieved from www.olt.gov.au.

Scott, G., Coates, H., and Anderson, M. (2008b). Learning leaders in times of change: Academic leadership capabilities for Australian higher education. *Australian Council for Educational Research.* Retrieved March 2018, from https://research.acer.edu.au/higher_education/3.

Smith, D.M. (2000). *Leadership and professional competencies: Serving higher education in an era of change.* Unpublished doctoral dissertation, University of Pennsylvania.

Snyder, H., Marginson, S., and Lewis, T. (2007). An alignment of the planets: Mapping the intersections between pedagogy, technology and management in Australian universities. *Journal of Higher Education Policy and Management*, 29(2), 1–16.

Spector, B.A. (2016). *Discourse on leadership: A critical appraisal*. New York, NY: Cambridge University Press.

Spillane, J. (2006). *Distributed leadership*. San Francisco, CA: Jossey-Bass.

Sternberg, R.J. (2015). *Academic leadership in higher education: From the top down and the bottom up*. Lanham: Rowman & Littlefield.

Stiles, D.R. (2004). Narcissus revisited: The values of management academics and their role in business school strategies in the UK and Canada. *British Journal of Management*, 15, 157–175.

St. John, E.P. and Parsons, M.D. (Eds.). (2004). *Public funding of higher education: Changing contexts and new rationales*. Baltimore: Johns Hopkins University Press.

Szekeres, J. (2006). General staff experiences in the corporate university. *Journal of Higher Education Policy and Management*, 26(2), 133–145.

Thomas, B. and Sweetman, L. (2018). *Exploring consensual leadership in higher education: Co-operation, collaboration and partnership*. Edited by Lynne Gornall. Perspectives on Leadership in Higher Education. London: Bloomsbury Academic.

Vilkinas, T. and Ladyshewsky, R. (2011). *Academic leadership development within the university sector by dissemination of a web-based 360° feedback process and related professional development workshops*. Report to Office for Learning and Teaching. Retrieved from www.olt.gov.au/resource?text=Vilkinas.

Waitere, H., Wright, J., Tremaine, M., Brown, S., and Pause, J. (2011). Choosing whether to resist or reinforce the new managerialism: The impact of performance-based research findings on academic identity. *Higher Education Research and Development*, 30(2), 205–217.

Wenger, E. (2000). *Communities of practice: Learning, meaning, and identity*. Cambridge, UK: Cambridge University Press.

Whitchurch, C. (2006). Who do they think they are? The changing identities of professional administrators and managers in UK higher education. *Journal of Higher Education Policy and Management*, 28(2), 159–171.

Whitchurch, C. (2008). Shifting identities and blurring boundaries: The emergence of third space professionals in UK Higher Education. *Higher Education Quarterly*, 62(4), 377–396.

Whitchurch, C. (2012). Expanding the parameters of academia. *Higher Education*, 64, 99–117.

Woods, P., Bennett, N., Harvey, J., and Wise, C. (2004). Variables and dualities in distributed leadership. *Educational Management Administration and Leadership*, 32(4), 439–457.

Woods, P. and Gronn, P. (2009). Nurturing democracy. *Educational Management Administration and Leadership*, 37(4), 430–451.

Yielder, J. and Codling, A. (2004). Management and leadership in the contemporary university. *Journal of Higher Education and Management*, 26(3), 315–328.

Zemsky, R. (2013). *Checklist for change: Making American higher education a sustainable enterprise*. New Brunswick, NJ: Rutgers University Press.

Index

Note: Page numbers in **bold** indicate tables and *italic* indicates figures.

Jazz at Lincoln Center 12
jazz music: art for art's sake concept
and 7; complexity of, increasing
6; dichotomy between joyful
experiences and stubborn realities
7; popularity of, decreasing 6,
8–9; programming time in past
8; reconnecting music with the
public and 6–7
job availability 32

Kant, Immanuel 70
Kaufmann, Jonas 74
Kellerman, Barbara 100–101, 106n12
Kotter, John **97**, 104–105n5
KPMG 65
Kremer, Gidon 7
Kremerata Baltica 7
Kübler-Ross, Elisabeth **97**, 105n6

Lane, Andrew **24**, 30, 40–42
leadership development,
partnerships with 101–102
Lewin, Kurt **97**, 104n4
live performance artists 12

McAlpin, C. 75
McAndrew, S. 73
McClary, S. 52
Mac Donald, Heather 15
McKinsey Global Institute report
(2018) 66
Malina, Stuart **24**, 31, 34, 36, 39–42
marketing skills 13, 50
Massive Open Online Courses
(MOOCs) 66
mentorships 11
Moody's Investor Service 63
music degrees, reshaping 9, 102
musicianship, reshaping definition
of 9–11
musicological approach 82n37
music performance-related
competencies, proposed 52, *52*
music skills/products, training
musicians with new **33**, 36–37
Myers, David **25**, 34, 93, 95

Nason, Rick 103
National Association of College
and University Business Officers
(NACUBO) 64

National Association for Music
Education (NAfME) 100, 105n10
National Association of Schools of
Music (NASM) 8, 62, 100
New Republic 74
Newton, Sir Isaac 70
nontraditional skills **38**, 40–42

Ohlsson, Garrick 42
Op.130 string quartet (Beethoven)
74
openness for career success 39–40,
39
Opera Philadelphia 10
organizational change models 96,
97–98, *99*
ownership for career success, taking
39, 40

Panay, Panos 12
partnerships: with industries that
employ music students 101;
with leadership development/
cultural experts 101–102; within
universities/colleges 13
pedagogical challenges for higher
education institutions **64**, 66
performance training: apprenticeship
72–73; art for art's sake concept
and 7–8; business skills and
13; careers and 8; conservatory
model 3, 6–7, 9; degrees,
reshaping 9; finance-oriented
skills and 13; gap between needs
of marketplace and classical
music 3; marketing skills and 13;
proposed orientation of music
performance-related competencies
52, *52*; student's personhood,
respect for 51; technology skills
and 12–13; traditional model
52; *see also* higher education
and classical music; performance
training changes, factors
thwarting; performance training
recommendations
performance training changes,
factors thwarting: background
information 62; combination
of factors 67–70, **68**; culture/
value system of classical music-
oriented programs/faculty 70–75;